THE QUEST

THE QUEST

Script of
Goutam Ghose's Film *Moner Manush*
Based on a novel by Sunil Gangopadhyay

Translated
from Bengali by Shankar Sen

NIYOGI
BOOKS

Published by

NIYOGI BOOKS
D-78, Okhla Industrial Area, Phase-I
New Delhi-110 020, INDIA
Tel: 91-11-26816301, 49327000
Fax: 91-11-26810483, 26813830
email: niyogibooks@gmail.com
website: www.niyogibooks.com

Editor: Mohua Mitra/Niyogi Books
Design: seema sethi {design}

ISBN: 978-93-81523-13-1
Publication: 2012

Printed at: Niyogi Offset Pvt. Ltd., New Delhi, India

Contents

Is the 'jol' above 'pani'
Or the 'pani' above 'jol' ...
Tell me, oh Khuda,
tell me, oh lord ...

Is Kali above Ali
Or Ali above Kali
Tell me, oh Khuda,
tell me, oh lord.

The earth lies below
and above floats the sky.
Or are they both set up
equally high ...
Tell me, oh Khuda,
tell me, oh lord.

In a cemetery a Hindu
is set on fire,
In a graveyard a Mian
is buried in earth
Tell me, which is higher,
tell me what each is worth.

Tell me, oh Khuda,
tell me, oh lord ...
Is the jol above pani
Or the pani above jol ...
Tell me, oh Khuda,
tell me, oh lord ...

Siraj Sain's song
(Scene 20, Shots 1-4)

Joler upor pani na panir upor jol ...
Bol Khoda bol Khoda bol ...
Alir upor Kali, na Kalir upor Ali
Bol Khoda, bol Khoda, bol ...
Jamin tolaye ashman upor
Naki ashman jamin shob borabor
Bol Khoda, bol Khoda, bol ...
Hindu pora shamshan aar miyanr gorasthan
Kahar theke ke chhoto kao, kar ki obosthan
Bol Khoda, bol Khoda, bol ...
Joler upor pani na panir upor jol ...
Bol Khoda, bol Khoda, bol ...

'A woman holds jealousy within herself and desire in her eyes

Introduction

The seeds of an idea for producing a film on *Moner Manush* were probably sown in 1989 while I was making a documentary on Bharatratna Ustad Bismillah Khan. Reminiscing on his youth Khan sahib had said, 'My brother and I used to bathe in the holy Ganga very early in the morning, read our *namaz* in the mosque and then go down to the Balaji temple where we played the *shenhai*. Life was very simple and happy.' When I heard this, I asked myself – was this simple way of life mentioned by Ustadji the mysterious, solitary path which every human being craved for? Khan sahib had also said, 'There are seven scales and five flat notes lie hidden in them. And it is in the combination of these seven scales and five notes that every single tune of this world is held. Music, my friend, has no caste or religion.' To me, Khan sahib had then seemed to stand out as a living symbol of the composite culture of this sub-continent.

The demolition of Babri Masjid occurred soon after that, followed by extensive communal riots. I was shocked and mortified like countless other people of this country. My first reaction was to produce a film on this devastating episode, but the next moment I realised that producing a film on a riot was nothing but displaying violence and blood-shed. Rather, it would be a far more responsible act to produce a film on a non-institutional and non-sectarian worshipper like Kabir or Lalon. I even set out to do some research on Lalon Fakir, but for various reasons it had not been possible to produce a film on Lalon at that time. Many years passed thereafter. With the advent of the new millennium the world seemed to be struck by an even stronger wave of intolerance, as if seized by a surge of prejudice in matters related to religion, politics and culture. I decided that it was the right time for launching my project on Lalon Fakir.

In its autumn issue of 2008 the Bengali magazine *Desh* brought out a novel on Lalon Fakir – *Moner Manush*, written by the renowned literateur, Sunil Gangopadhyay. Sunil-*da*'s writing filled me with a strong urge to

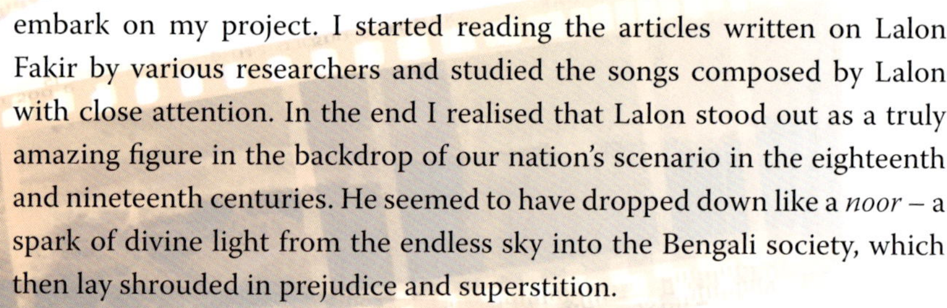

embark on my project. I started reading the articles written on Lalon Fakir by various researchers and studied the songs composed by Lalon with close attention. In the end I realised that Lalon stood out as a truly amazing figure in the backdrop of our nation's scenario in the eighteenth and nineteenth centuries. He seemed to have dropped down like a *noor* – a spark of divine light from the endless sky into the Bengali society, which then lay shrouded in prejudice and superstition.

Annada Shankar Roy had once written – 'Just as Ram Mohan Roy played an important role in the revival of Bengal, so did Lalon play a vital part in lighting up the minds of the common people with the joy and hope of a Diwali festival. We are overwhelmed by the enormous impact created by a single individual on the prevailing folk-culture of a country. And thus, while the educated urban society had started experiencing the reviving impact of renaissance the illiterate rural people were stirred by a different sort of emotion, the like of which they had never known before.'

The pundits are not in accord about Lalon's date of birth. But judging from the political scenario of his time we may assume that he was born shortly after the East India Company was granted the right of governance of Bengal, Bihar and Orissa. It would thus appear that Lalon's life had been spent through an important stage of British rule.

Radical changes in the land-system following the implementation of the Permanent Settlement had led to the birth of a new class of feudal lords. And it were these men, who founded the *babu* culture and remained its staunch patrons for generations thereafter. With the support of the British rulers they came to be identified as educated middle class Bengalis who thrived with the city of Calcutta as their nucleus.

English education and the influence of European authors and scientists had helped a few Indians to unearth certain ancient theories and past glories with the support of foreign experts and thereby raise a spirit of reawakening in their society. But that spirit had failed to gain entry into the non-communal consciousness of the general public. On one hand there was the ultra-conservative outlook of the illiterate Bengali Muslims, who had been denied the benefit of modern education and on the other hand there was the gross neglect and indifference in which they were held by the Bengali Hindus, who staunchly stood for separatism in religious faiths. These realities posed severe constraints before the Bengali Muslims in taking part in the reawakening. But then, this reawakening was not an outcome of any joint effort of Hindus and Muslims nor had it brought them in close harmony. Rather, it had served to make the conflicts, differences and many disparities between the two communities even more pronounced. And thus, even today the dictionary of Bengali language is divided – one dominated by Persian and Arabic and the other by Sanskrit. The fact remains, however, that Bengali language was originally derived from **Prakrit*, but had been joined later by Persian, Arabic and Turkish words and eventually by Sanskrit as well, all of which had occurred due to historic reasons.

Side by side with the renaissance in the urban population another reawakening was occurring among the people living in the rural and suburban areas of Bengal. This emergence had found particular support in Lalon's practices and songs, which had served to bring the people of rural Bengal closer and united them into a single unit, irrespective of caste or religion. There were thus no divisions in Lalon's dictionary and a larger and far expanded Bengali language had gained its birth by a mingling of its original version with Persian, Arabic, Turkish and Sanskrit words and expressions.

It is heard that Lalon was an illiterate man. But going through the words of his songs and their implied significance it seems as if he was an erudite scholar, tutored in an age-old system of education. Lalon's religious thoughts used to find expression in his songs, which carried the radiance of a very deep philosophy. His faith was not guided by any particular religion. Rather, it could be said to comprise the mysticism of Sufi, the love and forgiveness of Vaishnavism and the liberal spirit of the *Tantrik* sect of Budddhism, which allowed a devotee to act as per his instincts. I am inclined to accept the views expressed in this regard by Annada Shankar Roy who had once said –'The main stream, I believe, is Buddhist liberalism, with Islamic Sufi and Vaishnavism running alongside. These three streams had united in Lalon's religious pursuit and in his thoughts and actions. In fact, Buddhist liberalism had created a field for religious pursuit since long, which is evident from the *Charjyapada* – lyrics composed by the liberal Buddhist sect.

Lalon's religious quest was undertaken through the medium of human beings. Lalon's religious practices were not organised in any established

My caste is lost, oh my caste is lost –
It's really a strange business!
There is no one who wants to work for truth,
All they know is tum-tess titum-tess...
What was your caste when you came here,
What caste did you take on arrival, dear,
What would be your caste when it's time to go -
Ponder and tell me if you know.
A Brahmin, a scavenger, a low-born squatter
All become purified by a drop of the same water.
As I see this, I am filled with disgust and mutter—
Death won't spare anyone, nevertheless ...

Jaat galo jaat galo boley eki ajob karkhana
Shotyo kaajey keu noy raaji shob dekhi ta-na-na-na-na
Ashbar kaaley ki jaat chhiley
Eshey tumi ki jaat niley
Ki jaat hoba jabar kaaley
Shey kotha bhebey bolona
Brahman-chandaal-chamaar-muchi
Ek joley hoy shob go shuchi
Dekhey shuney hoyna ruchi,
Jomey to kauke chhharbey na

Scene 40, Shot 11

Nikon
Lee

pattern, which is why he had been the victim of contempt, vilification and enmity of both Hindus and Muslims all through his life.

In the words of Abul Ahsan, eminent researcher on Lalon Fakir – 'Time and again his religion of love had been subjected to reproach and humiliation by the religious Gurus who were well-versed in scriptures and by the then heads of society. But Lalon had progressed in a calm and composed manner towards his destination, undeterred by any handicap and unmoved by any constraint. Just as a river runs ceaselessly towards the sea passing over all obstacles, so had Lalon Fakir ignored all animosities and moved steadily towards what he believed to be the truth, looking for the single entity which his heart craved for. Lalon was a seeker of truth, which is why any personal feelings caused by those repeated blows were not reflected anywhere in his songs.'

The *Baul* community had renounced all recognised institutional religions and revolted against long-established rites, customs and faiths. Breaking down the barriers of the narrow confines of communal faith they had found a large expanse under the sky, which had served as a bountiful meeting place of many religions. Counted as one of the principal folk-groups of Bengal, the *Baul* community composed its own songs, which symbolised devotional lyrics and were aimed to expound the deep mystery of the *Baul* religious culture to followers and disciples. No conscious effort to create any artistic effect was found in those songs.This latter feature was also noticeable in the songs sung by Lalon Fakir, who did not compose his songs out of any artistic design but with the sole objective of providing benefit to his followers. And yet, by virtue of their deep sensitivity and emotional appeal those songs had crossed the ambits of objectives and necessity to enter the select circle of artistic creations. Lalon's songs were thus devotional lyrics on one hand and on the other hand, they carried deep philosophical annotations in addition to being poetic creations embellished with an artist's passion.

The life-story of this ever-compassionate devotee, who preferred to remain immersed in himself and was totally averse to publicity – is shrouded in mystery. And because no description of the successive events of his life were available, the chroniclers had to rely on heresay and assumptions in several places. But nevertheless, the researchers who devoted themselves to finding out about the life and teachings of

Lalon Fakir from the later period of the nineteenth century till this day have done a most commendable job. Although they are divided in their views on many matters there is no dispute among them on two pieces of documentary evidence. One is an article which appeared after Lalon's death in a periodical named *Hitakari* on 31 October 1890 and the other is a portrait of Lalon Fakir in an advanced age, drawn by Jyotirindranath Tagore, elder brother of the poet Rabindranath. Incidentally, Lalon's hamlet was located in the forest of the Chheuria area, which fell within the *zamindari* of the Tagore family.

While I was composing the film-script it had struck me that Lalon Fakir had visited the house-boat of Jyotirindranath Tagore at the latter's invitation, when his portrait was drawn. At that time there must have been some interaction between the two, one – a young man, enlightened and highly educated in the prevailing tradition and the other – an ancient sage, who had no book-learning. It is based on this assumption that I had drawn up the script of *Moner Manush*. Sunil Gangopadhyay had based his novel on the findings of many researchers, some assumptions and on his own perception of Lalon's songs. And based on Sunil-*da*'s novel with the added input of my own understanding and thoughts, I have tried to compose this film-script in the language of cinema.

It is often seen that when a film is produced on the basis of a published work of fiction the viewers have a tendency to compare the film with the text of the original novel. In reality, such comparison is in no way feasible, because literature is not translated into a film, rather, it is transformed into a motion picture and in the process, the author's feelings and experience merge with the feelings and experience of the film-maker. Just as literature has its own language and grammar so too does a film have its separate language and grammar. Then again, the perceptions of a reader and a viewer in their reading and viewing are different. When we read something the words, the sounds and the sentences enter our intellectual perception first and then the visual perception is formed, with each reader creating his own image in his mind. But just the opposite happens in a cinema. The moving picture enters our visual perception and then we apply our intellectual perception to understand its meaning and grasp its significance. Thus an expression of literature can never be used as an expression in a film, rather, it has to be given a new cinematographic form if necessary.

The film-script of *Moner Manush* is not a biography of Lalon Fakir. The successive stages of Lalon's emergence as Lalon Fakir, the then prevailing social scenario, a disciple's unwavering faith in his Guru and a man's endless journey in quest of the single entity that his heart craves for—all this is brought out through the interaction between Lalon and Jyotirindranath Tagore. In a particular scene of the film, Jyotirindranath asks Lalon curiously, 'Are you people liberalists?' To which Lalon replies, 'We are a rudderless raft in a shoreless river. You can call us a hidden current too—those who want to get lost with us, can get lost.'

This 'hidden current' was a truly wonderful treasure of our rural Bengal. It was literally *a fair of joy* for people, who were uplifted, broadminded and non-communal in spirit and were yet treated as outcastes by their society. The human society of today – dissolute, intolerant and avaricious as they are – has much to learn from the easy way of life of those *baul*-fakirs. In his introduction to Muhammad Mansaruddin's *Haramoni*, Rabindranath Tagore had written, 'People, who declare themselves as well-educated in our country, are often driven by their own needs to go round looking for many devices for uniting the Hindus and Muslims. But they are educated in the history-schools of other countries and have not cared to learn the history of their own country—a land, where the spirit of that very union has been borne all along in the deep truth prevailing in the minds of the people. In *Baul* literature and the lifestyle of the *Baul* community I can see how Hindus and Muslims had been united through a single pursuit, but neither community had hurt the other. This union had not been brought about by meetings or conferences, nor had it led to such deliberations. But, on the other hand, it had given birth to many beautiful songs—songs bearing words and tunes, which were rich with the charm of raw artlessness. The words and tunes of these songs had drawn the Hindus and Muslims close to each other without raising any dispute between the Koran and the Hindu scriptures. It was a union which stood out as a true symbol of India's civilisation.'

Lalon used to sing:
'*Why do you ask about Khuda,*
pointing towards the sky?
He has no one of his own,

and no one knows why.
The earth is round, I am told,
rotating all the time and behold,
how it makes day, followed by night—,
wise men say so and they must be right.'

This song made me wonder how Lalon could have come to know about the rotation of the earth. He could not have read the works of Copernicus or Galileo. But then, I remembered that the science of astronomy had been handed down by word of mouth from generation to generation in ancient India. Today, driven by the arrogance of our English education we have come to ignore our popular folk-lores and we have looked down upon the *Baul* fakirs, addressing them as corrupt debauches belonging to the lowest scum of society. But the time has now come to make amends for our mistakes, to revive our heritage and restore our lost culture. The film *Moner Manush* is a step in that direction—an invitation to adopt the non-communal, liberal and human attitude of Lalon Fakir in our own lives and thoughts. In the words of Lalon –

'When will the rains arrive?
It is with that single hope that I thrive.'

The cinematic adaption of the story has been reproduced in this book as a film-script and not as a literary narrative. I have been writing shot-wise scripts for the last fifteen years by planning the sequence in which the scenes have to be shot for producing the film. Needless to say, changes are made if found necessary while the shooting is in progress. In recent years I have come to notice a growing curiosity among knowledgeable viewers about the many technical details of film-making. An index of abbreviated technical terms has, therefore, been provided at the commencement of the script and I hope that the readers would be able to feel the camera's eye with the rhythm of the film which should make the reading of this book even more enjoyable.

In the composition of this film-script I received unstinted cooperation from the eminent author, Sahjad Firdous and also from Sabyasachi Mukherjee, who helped me all along while I was occupied in this work.

I acknowledge my deep gratitude to both of them. The author Sunil Gangopadhyay was delighted to read the film-script and he gave me some valuable advice.

Shankar Sen was overwhelmed after watching *Moner Manush* and when I read some of his spontaneous English translations of Lalon's songs, I realised that he was the right person for bringing out the passion and significance of the film-script. These impressions were confirmed when I read his finished manuscript and I must add here that it is only through Shankar-*da*'s initiative that this English translation of the script of *Moner Manush* is ready for publication soon after the release of the film.

Last but not the least I shall remain ever grateful to Niyogi Books for the meticulous care which they have taken in publishing this book.

Kolkata,
March 2012 Goutam Ghose

* Prakrit: *A language derived from Vedic Sanskrit – which became extinct in later periods – in which men and women had equal rights and equal freedom and where the adoration of the human body was neither based on inclination nor derived from renunciation, rather it was built on a consensual spirit and a bond of like-mindedness, but that too involved an austere religious practice.'*

When shall I be united with the single entity
For whom my heart pines with such intensity?
Like a thirsty cuckoo I fix my sight
On the dark moon as I pine all night
To serve at the feet of the one I adore –
Alas, I am denied by fate as I was denied before.

Lalon's song
(Scene 68, Shot-3)

Milon hobey koto diney
Amar moner manusheri shoney
Chatok praye aharnishi
Cheye achhe kal shoshi
Hobo bole choron dashi
O ta hoyna kopal guney

'To look for oneself is looking for the other.
Looking for the other is looking for all.
Looking for all is looking for God.

– Lalon Fakir

Translator's Note

I was invited to a special screening of *Moner Manush* at Dhaka in August 2010 by my friends, Habibur Rahman Khan and Faridur Reza Sagor, who had co-produced the film. I am not a regular movie-goer these days, but this was one of those rare films which had me glued to my seat all through and left me hoping that something more was going to be shown even as the end title was fading out on the screen. Apart from some enthralling scenery captured by brilliant camera-work what fascinated me were the dialogues and songs, which seemed simple and yet deeply significant in today's scenario.

I asked Habib Bhai if he could let me read the film-script, which he did soon after the film was released in December 2010 and at his suggestion I started translating the script in English. It was only then that I realised that what had seemed to be plain and lucid was, in fact, intense and profound with hidden meanings which came to light only after close application. Habib introduced me to Goutam Ghose and I found that here was a man who was still living in the world of *Moner Manush*—engrossed in the words, phrases and songs that he had composed. For the first time in my life I had a glimpse of the depth to which a dedicated artist could become absorbed in his own creation.

I had by then drawn up my own interpretations of Lalon's songs and dialogues, but after my discussions with Goutam I sat down to rewrite almost everything that I had written. And when the translation was eventually finished I still could not resist the urge to make changes here and there every time I read it. To be honest, I cannot really claim even now that this is a *done* job, because I have a feeling that there are many thoughts which I might have left unexplored, many similes which I might not have interpreted correctly and many expressions which I might have failed to reproduce as they should have been.

I am not a religious man. My religious breeding, if I may call it so, was mixed. My grandfather was born in a staunch Brahmin family but he chose to embrace Brahmhoism in his youth and served as an *Acharya* of the Brahmo Samaj till his last day. My mother was a disciple of Rama Krishna Mission. I was brought up in a catholic school and had been a firm believer in the Bible till my adolescence when my mother made me study the *Geeta, Chandi* and *Ramakrishna Kathamrita*. Perhaps, in some ways this mixed religious background has helped me to appreciate the philosophy of Lalon Fakir's teachings. And it even prompts me to go a step forward and think that just as the present generation of young people have acquired a right to choose their careers and future professions, a privilege which was denied to most of us in our youth, who knows – maybe the generations that are still to come might exercise their right to choose which religion they were going to pursue – thereby putting an end to the many invisible barriers which now divide the population of this world. And maybe, some of them might even decide to adopt the *religion of humanity* and set out to search the single entity which their heart craved for. Lalon Fakir may then gain immortality and the creators of *Moner Manush* may rest content that their mission has been truly accomplished.

Shankar Sen
Kolkata, March 2012

List of Abbreviations used in the Film Script of The Quest (*Moner Manush*)

Abbreviation	Full expression
SC	Scene
C.S.	Close Shot
L.S.	Long Shot
M.S.	Mid Shot
M.C.S.	Mid Close Shot
M.L.S.	Mid Long Shot
P.O.V.	Point Of View

Above, right and extreme right: Location shots from *Moner Manush (The Quest)* while setting up camera and lighting equipment by the riverside. The film has made extensive use of rivers, ranging from sweeping shots to close-ups

Left: Camera on crane at water level with the sun setting on the opposite bank. Picturisation of the opening shot of the film

SC No.	SHOT	DESCRIPTION & DIALOGUE
		The Opening Title Card on Black Background -5Nos.
1.	1.	**Location: River bank** **Time : Sunset** **Camera on Crane: Long focus lens** **Title Scene.** Camera on water-level. Sun setting in the horizon on the opposite bank. A raft made of banana stalks tied together comes floating from one end of the Frame. A fishing net is hung across four bamboo twigs fixed to four corners of the raft. A dead body lies in the net. The body cannot be recognised in the fading light of the evening; the raft floats away slowly and passes beyond the Frame. Meanwhile the sun sinks gradually in the western horizon. A muezzin's call to attend evening prayers comes floating from a distant mosque. Camera crane is progressively raised. The Title is super-imposed. The muezzin's call and the Title display are concluded at the same time. Superimposed Title Card 23 Nos.
		FADE OUT
2.	1.	**Location: Padma or Garhai river** **Time: Afternoon** **M.L.S.** A house-boat is moving on the river. A flock of storks is seen flying across the water. In the background of the water there is a long stretch of sandy land.
		CUT
	2	**M.S. to C.S. (on trolley)** Inside the house-boat.

An aged man, looking like a fakir is seen sitting on a chair. He has long, curly hair, flowing down his neck. His beard is partly grey. He is holding a stick lightly in his left hand. A bundle belonging to the fakir is kept beside his chair. Part of a single-stringed lute sticks out of the bundle.

The old fakir's profile. He is leaning slightly forward in his chair. His eyes are stretched towards the far distance in a blank stare. A boat passes by with colourful sails.

The old fakir shifts in his chair, turns his face around once to look towards the left of the Camera. Jyotirindra's Off Voice is heard from the left.

SC No.	SHOT	DESCRIPTION & DIALOGUE

Jyotirindranath: You are feeling a little weary perhaps. Fakir sahib, I am sorry that I have put you into discomfort.

The Camera tracks to Jyoti Thakur and brings him in the Frame with back to Camera. Before him there is a sketch-book placed on an easel. Jyoti Thakur goes on sketching as he says –

Jyotirindranath: Since my childhood I have had this fancy for capturing people of various types in my sketch-book. Portrait drawing – was not known in Bengal earlier. It was introduced here after the arrival of the British …

3 M.S.

Jyotiridranath: Even a low- ranked soldier of the East India Company can sketch. Strange, isn't it? … Our family has started taking interest in the devotional songs that you sing. They are very enthusiastic and they have many questions about you. And now they will all be delighted when they see your portrait.

The old fakir smiles briefly and says –

Lalon: But, my feet are getting cramped, *Babu Moshai.

CUT

4 M.C.S.

In the frame – Jyoti Thakur's face appears through a gap in a part of the easel.

He is a good-looking young man.

Jyotirindranath: All right. Take a little rest. We can resume later … I must confess that I am particularly keen to learn about your ways of meditation and worship. People talk of so many things, but I cannot believe everything that they say … I am left with many questions, which is why I want to hear about them from you.

CUT

* Babu Moshai: A term of respect for addressing a highly-placed gentleman

SC No.	SHOT	DESCRIPTION & DIALOGUE

5 **M.C.S**

Lalon smiles briefly and starts humming to himself.
Lalon: *Do not go on talking of your worship here and there. Keep your thoughts to yourself and always beware . . .*

CUT

6 **M.C.S**

Jyotirindranath is surprised to hear Lalon's verse. He gets immersed in thoughts as he concentrates on his painting.

CUT

7 **C.S.**

The ink darkens on a particular spot of the sketch under Jyotirindranath's hand.
On the easel lies the sketch book with Lalon Fakir's incomplete sketch.

DISSOLVE . . .

Unknowingly I tasted a wild arum and now
I must get some tamarind right away somehow...
Arum has a terrible itch, as everyone knows,
But this I had sadly failed to diagnose.
Now I am driven mad by its burning trek,
My throat's itching without a moment's break.

Kheyechhi be-jetey kochu na bujhey
Ekhon tentul kotha pai khunjey
Kochu emon maan goshain
Tarey chinley naarey bhai
Kheye holum pagol para
Ekhon chupni ghora chulkaichhey

Scene 63, Shot 4-5

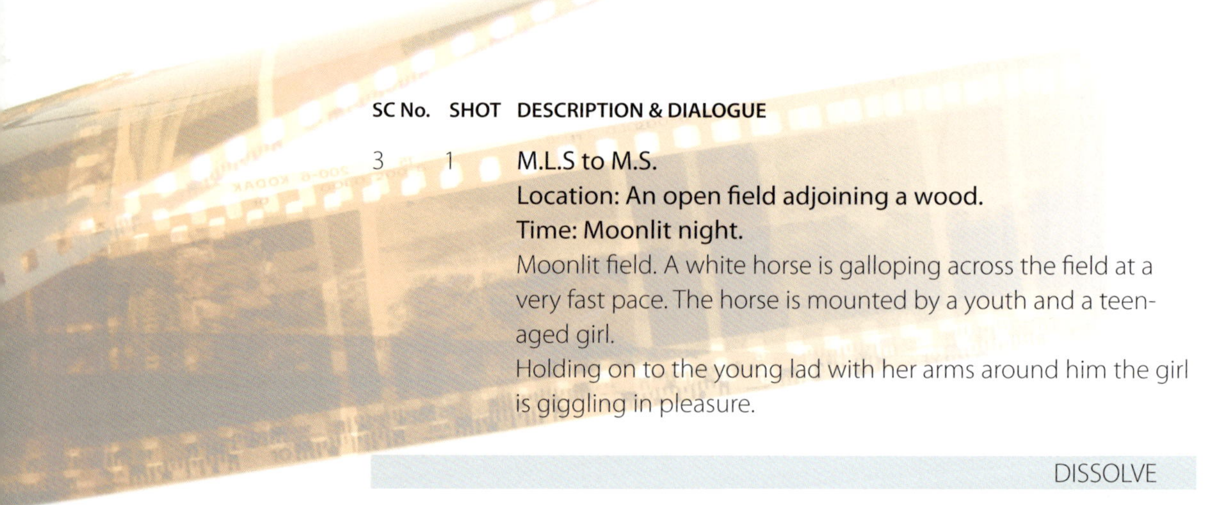

SC No.	SHOT	DESCRIPTION & DIALOGUE
3	1	**M.L.S to M.S.** **Location: An open field adjoining a wood.** **Time: Moonlit night.** Moonlit field. A white horse is galloping across the field at a very fast pace. The horse is mounted by a youth and a teen-aged girl. Holding on to the young lad with her arms around him the girl is giggling in pleasure.

DISSOLVE

SC No. SHOT DESCRIPTION & DIALOGUE

SC No.	SHOT	DESCRIPTION & DIALOGUE
4	1	Location: A pond surrounded by palm trees Time: Morning M.L.S. (Toppish) A still pond surrounded by palm trees. There is a soft sound and ripples appear on the water-surface. A fruit might have fallen from some tree or a fish might have struck the water with its tail from below.
	2	M.S. Lalu sits by the pond, looking in wonder at the ripples.
		CUT
	3	M.C.S. Lalu's P.O.V. The shapes are changing in many ways on the water surface. Lalu starts humming a song – **Lalu (Song)**: *Who made those ripples on the water?*
		CUT

SC No. SHOT DESCRIPTION & DIALOGUE

4 **(Same as Shot-2) M.C.S.**
Lalu hums a song as he looks at the ripples on the water
Lalu (Song): *What does he look like, what is his colour,*
where does he dwell?
I cannot see him, I cannot touch him
and yet, I can hear him so well.

CUT

5 While Lalu hums the song his wife Golapi arrives, bearing a pitcher on her waist and stands beside him. Lalu looks at Golapi and says –

Lalu: No, dear wife, it did not work out, it did not work out well.

Golapi: God help me! You are sitting here and composing songs while the devil is waiting for you at home.

Lalu: What nonsense! What are you babbling about?

Golapi places the pitcher on the ground and flops down beside Lalu.

Golapi: *Kabiraj Moshai has summoned you. His footman Jadu has come to fetch you; he says that Kabiraj Moshai is

* Kabiraj: A physician who follows the Ayurvedic system of treatment
* Moshai: Abbreviation of Mahashay, a term of courtesy affixed to a gentleman's name

SC No. SHOT DESCRIPTION & DIALOGUE

determined to take out every single worm from your brain.
Now, everyone has come to know of our secret, my dear ...
Golapi bursts into tears as she says this.

CUT

6 **Lalu**: What does it matter? I'll tell them the truth.
Can't we even dream because we are poor?
There is another splashing sound on the water.
Lalu's eyes are drawn towards it.

CUT

7 **M.S.**
Lalu's P.O.V. Reflected on the rippling surface of the water.

CUT

5 1 **Location: The mansion of Kabiraj Krishna Prasanna Sen.**
Time: Morning
M.L.S. (Toppish)
Outer portion of the Kabiraj's mansion. A white horse is tied to a post in the open courtyard. Employees, servants and maids are seen in the courtyard, discharging their duties. Quite a few

SC No.	SHOT	DESCRIPTION & DIALOGUE

people are sitting on one side, waiting to escort the Kabiraj to their homes for treating patients. The Kabiraj is sitting on the veranda, smoking from a hubble-bubble.
Jadu and Lalu make their entrance.

CUT

2 **M.S. Composite**

The Kabiraj is speaking to a patient about her medicine and diet as Jadu escorts Lalu into the courtyard. Lalu bows down low and makes his obeisance to the Kabiraj from a distance.

Kabiraj: Bina – let somebody call Bina here.

CUT

3 **M.S. Composite**

The Kabiraj's wife, Giribala is sitting on a veranda in the inner sanctum of the mansion. Bina, her ten-year old maid is applying *alta* (lac-dye) on the borders of her feet.

Giribala: That's enough. Now go. The master has called you outside.

Bina keeps sitting in silence.

Giribala: What's wrong? You seem to have shrunk into a shell. Are you going to move?

CUT

4 **M.S. to M.C.S. (Long focus lens)**

Bina in Frame. Her face showing diffidence, Bina walks with slow steps towards her master.

Bina stops on reaching M.C.S.

Kabiraj: Do you know this fellow?

Bina: Oh yes, master. He played the role of Nitai in the opera held at Netya-babu's place on the full moon night of Dol-jatra. He danced so beautifully with his arms raised high! And he can sing very well too.

CUT

5 **M.S. Composite (on trolley)**

Kabiraj, Lalu and Bina, The Kabiraj scolds Bina as he says –

Kabiraj: Wretched girl, did I ask you if he can sing?
Tell me if you saw him stealing my horse last night . . .

Lalu: Master, I swear I did not steal your horse. I had come to return it.

On hearing this there is a wave of laughter among all those who are present. The Kabiraj too breaks into a smile as he says–

Kabiraj: What are you trying to tell me? The horse is mine – did I ever give it to you that you would return it –

The footman Jadu scolds Lalu as he says –

Jadu: Shut up! We saw you untying the rope.

Lalu replies in a calm voice –

Lalu: No, you did not. When I took it the horse was untethered ...

On hearing Lalu's statement the Kabiraj is seized by doubts.

The Camera tracks to reach the Kabiraj's M.C.S. Without looking at Jadu, the Kabiraj says –

Kabiraj: Jadu, fetch Abdul here.

Then he addresses Lalu—

Kabiraj: Come, Lalu, mount the horse and show everybody how you can ride. My Rani does not allow strangers to mount her.

CUT

SC No. SHOT DESCRIPTION & DIALOGUE

6 **(Same as Shot-4) M.L.S. (Toppish)**
Lalu walks confidently towards the horse. The whole lot of people in the courtyard have their eyes fixed on Lalu. He places his hand on the horse's dewlap, fondles her and then suddenly jumps up on to her back. Now Rani starts moving.

CUT

7 **C.S.**
The maid Bina goes on looking at Lalu with fascinated eyes. The singer Lalu is now transformed into a horse-rider.

8 **Camera on Crane [Ramp 32 FPS to 24 FPS]**
Lalu is encircling the courtyard on the horse.
His appearance seems to have changed all of a sudden.

The Camera follows him at a low angle.
For a moment the Camera becomes still. Lalu goes out of the Frame with the horse.
In his excitement the Kabiraj gets up from his chair and steps down from the veranda. The sound of the horse coming to a halt is heard.
Off Frame. Lalu advances on foot towards the Kabiraj, holding the horse by its reins. **Camera Crane is up.** Lalu draws near the Kabiraj and bows down to make his obeisance. Abdul comes and takes Rani's reins.

SC No.	SHOT	DESCRIPTION & DIALOGUE

Kabiraj: Now tell me, where do you go with the horse?

Lalu: I do not go anywhere, master. With my wife Golapi beside me I roam around in open fields and woodlands. Oh, we enjoy it so much!

Kabiraj: Wonderful! I spend two hundred maunds of my best paddy to buy the horse so that Lalu and his wife Golapi can ride it for their pleasure! You are truly brilliant!

Lalu breaks into a smile on hearing the Kabiraj's concluding comment. It is an innocent smile.

Kabiraj: Listen. You stupid oaf, what has happened to you is known as a poor man's horse-disease. It is an ailment which has no symptoms –

CUT

9 **M.S. Composite**

The Kabiraj stands up straight from his leaning position.

Kabiraj: I am giving you a light punishment today. You will chop the tree felled by the storm, which is lying by the marsh. Yes, that is your punishment.

CUT

Director's act: Goutam Ghose acts out the scene for Tathoi (Golapi)—approaching Lalu with food and water

SC No.	SHOT	DESCRIPTION & DIALOGUE
6	1	**Location: Beside the marsh** **Time: Late evening** **M.L.S.** Lalu is chopping the tree.
	2	**M.L.S. to M.C.S.** Golapi is seen advancing with a plate containing food in her hand. The sound of chopping wood is heard Off Frame. Golapi comes and stands in front of Camera. Her face is downcast.
		CUT
	3	**M.S.Composite** Lalu has chopped off most of the tree. Golapi enters the Frame bearing food on a plate and a pot of water. Lalu stops chopping. Sweat is running down freely all over his body. Taking the pot from Golapi Lalu gulps down the water. Seeing Lalu's condition Golapi starts sobbing. **Golapi**: You did not steal or rob and yet you are being punished for no reason. What sort of justice is this? **Lalu**: This is known as a poor man's punishment for horse-disease. Do you understand? Golapi uses the border of her sari to wipe the sweat from Lalu's forehead, face and body Sound of a single-stringed lute is heard on the Sound Track.
		CUT
7	1	**Location: Under a banyan tree by the marsh** **Time: Fading evening** **M.S.** A light mist has descended on the marsh. Under the tree a fakir is playing a one-stringed lute and singing all by himself. **Fakir (Song):** *Just on two wheels my car still runs its course,* *On it *Sain, you have built a house of three floors;*

SC No. **SHOT** **DESCRIPTION & DIALOGUE**

On canals, land and marshes the car moves with ease
And at noon it stops to bathe at any place I please . . .

CUT

2 **M.S. Composite to M.L.S. Composite**

Golapi is setting up the plate of food and the pot.of water. Lalu says –

Lalu: You may go home. I am going to make my obeisance to Gosainji.

Golapi: Wouldn't you eat anything?

Lalu advances towards the fakir. While still moving he says –

Lalu: I am not hungry.

Golapi: But don't be late.

Lalu advances towards the banyan tree. **Camera pans. Fakir comes within Frame.**

Fakir (Song):

Oh, Sain, my respected Guru, my lord and master,
Please tell me where I can dump this enormous monster;
Under its load I can feel my car totter and sway
I do not know what to keep and what to throw away.

CUT

3 **M.S. Composite**

Fakir finishes his song and goes on strumming his single-stringed lute. Lalu bends down to touch his feet in *pranam*. Fakir smiles and places his hand on Lalu's head.

Fakir: What is your name, lad?

Lalu: Lalonchandra Kar, sir.

Fakir: That's a nice name. Tell me, son, can you read and write? Do you go to school?

Lalu: Sir, we are very poor.

Fakir: Stupid boy! Being poor has nothing to do with it. In this world everyone is poor, everyone is a fakir, everyone a destitute—but why should that stop us from learning to read and write?

Lalu: I have no father . . .

* Sain: Revered Guru

SC No. **SHOT** **DESCRIPTION & DIALOGUE**

Fakir: So what! In this world everyone is helpless, everyone is an orphan, no one has a father –

At a distance a young girl is driving a pack of ducks across the marsh towards her home. Fakir Siraj Sain starts putting his one-stringed lute back in his bag, as he says –

Fakir: Son, I have to leave now. I must reach Chhaprha before it gets dark.

Fakir gets to his feet.

CUT

4 **M.S. (Long focus lens)**

Half Silhouette Fakir enters the Frame accompanied by Lalu.

Camera follows them.

Lalu: May I tell you something? I could not understand the meaning of your song…

Fakir: The meaning of my song? Barring idiots none else searches for the meaning of songs…

Lalu: Sainji, I want to become your disciple. Please tell me the meaning of your song and explain it to me a bit.

Fakir: I am nobody's disciple, nor do I have any disciple. I am only a servant of Alek Sain.

Lalu: What is the meaning of Alek?

Fakir: Again you want to know a meaning! Alek means that which remains hidden – does not appear before our eyes.

Fakir comes to a halt while saying this.

5 **M.C.S. (Composite)**

Suddenly a gust of wind tousles the Fakir's hair

Fakir: Listen, it is not very difficult to understand the meaning of the song I sang; but the song carries a lot of power which is difficult to hold on to…

Lalu: I do not understand you.

Fakir: Two wheels and a car – means two legs. On which there is a house of three floors, meaning the tummy, the chest and the head. And the bottom floor of this house is filled with rubbish, meaning all that is held in the tummy.
Have you understood anything? What is this car?

Lalu: Shall I tell you then?

SC No. SHOT DESCRIPTION & DIALOGUE

Fakir: Tell me.

Lalu makes signs to draw a human body.

Fakir: You have got it perfectly right … now your brain is working … the next words are – the human chest is the real place, the true domain, that is where gold, silver and costly jewels are held. Search the chest and you will find a man's most valuable possessions hidden there. But the problem is that it is so difficult to carry the weight of a three-storied house on just two wheels. And so my car totters and is on the verge of collapse all the time.

CUT

6 **L.S.**

Lalu prostrates himself on the ground before the fakir in *pranam*. The rumbling sound of clouds is heard on the Sound track.

CUT

View through the lens: Director and camera crew taking a top view in the forest location in north Bengal

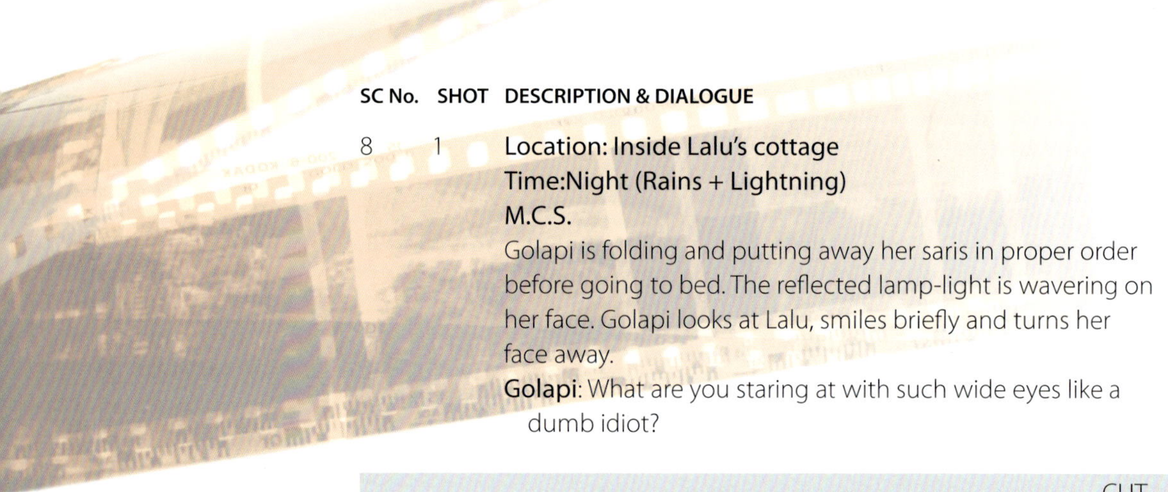

SC No.	SHOT	DESCRIPTION & DIALOGUE
8	1	**Location: Inside Lalu's cottage** **Time:Night (Rains + Lightning)** **M.C.S.** Golapi is folding and putting away her saris in proper order before going to bed. The reflected lamp-light is wavering on her face. Golapi looks at Lalu, smiles briefly and turns her face away. **Golapi**: What are you staring at with such wide eyes like a dumb idiot?

CUT

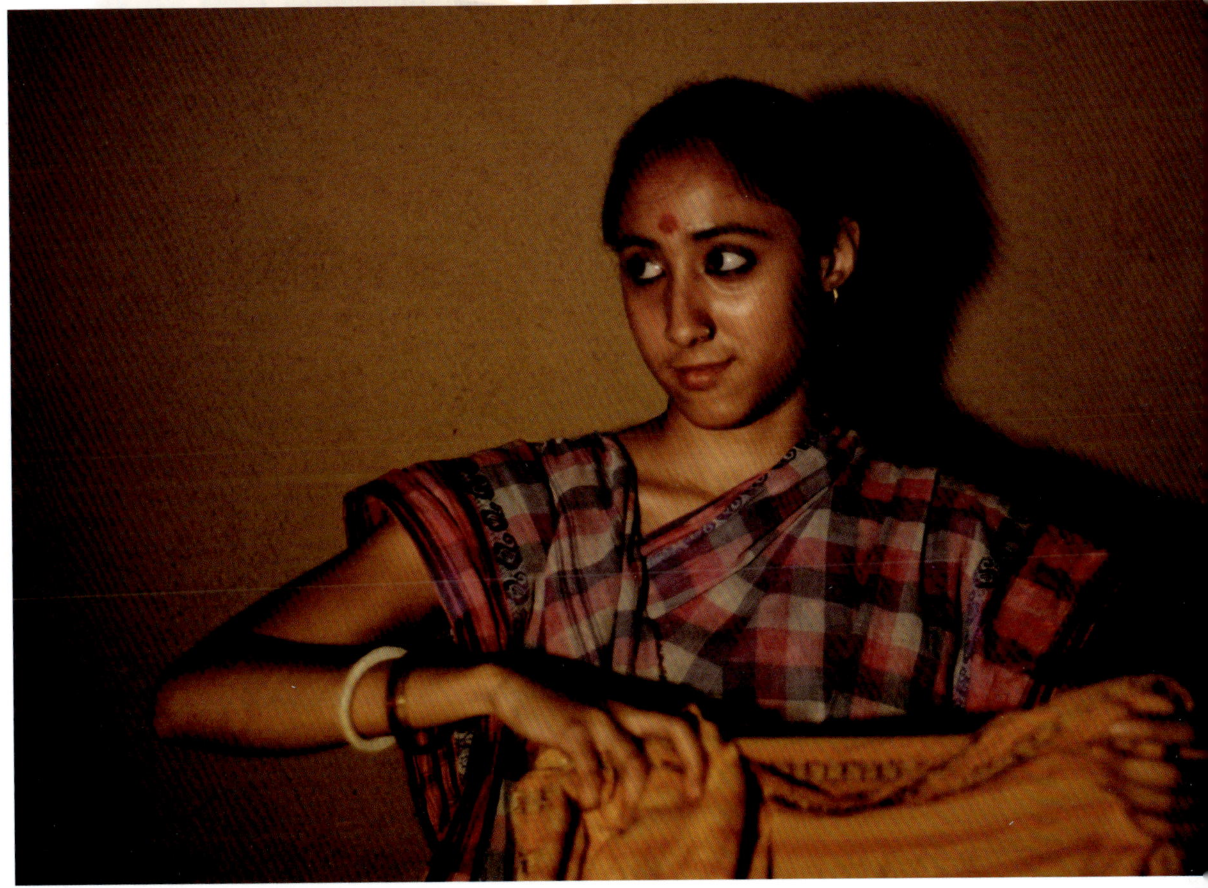

2 **M.C.S. (House boat)**

The last fading light of the day is seen reflected on the face of old Lalon. Unconsciously a word slips from his mouth.

Lalon: You …

CUT

SC No.	SHOT	DESCRIPTION & DIALOGUE

Between the shots: Actors Naufel Jishan and Tathoi playing Lalon and Golapi respectively, take a break

3 **Cottage/Night**

Golapi makes a face and says –

Golapi: What is there to see in me? You see me every day, don't you?

CUT

4 **M.C.S. (House Boat)**

Lalon: I see you every day and yet I want to see you … The more I see you the more I search …

CUT

5 **Cottage/Night**

Golapi: You are a lubberly fish – I can make no sense of what you say –

CUT

6 **M.C.S. (House boat)**

Lalon: You are right. I am a lubberly fish … and you are a puny fish …

After saying this he starts humming a song.

Lalu (Song):

A puny fish jumped up from the pond too soon
At an odd hour on a Saturday afternoon …

CUT

SC No.	SHOT	DESCRIPTION & DIALOGUE
	7	**M.S. Composite** **Camera on trolley** **Cottage/Night** Lalu sings as he lies half-stretched out on a coarse mattress of date-leaves.

Lalu (Song):
So ripples after ripples rose upon the water-bed.
And to the woods, eluding me, my mind's bird fled.
Ripples after ripples made the water-bed sway.
What trick did my mind's bird play as it flew away?

Golapi is brought in the Frame. She sits very close to Lalu. Camera tracks to catch Golapi in preference and Lalu in suggestion. Golapi speaks out in an overwhelmed voice –

Golapi: Are you a minstrel-fakir – that you can compose songs with every word?
Tell me who you really are.

CUT

8 **M.C.S. (House boat)**

Old Lalon looks out listlessly. A single tear trickles down his eye.

CUT

9 1 **Location: Lalu's Cottage**
Time: Morning
M.S. Composite.

Lalu crosses the courtyard and walks towards the kitchen, carrying a bunch of dried branches. His mother Padmabati is screening rice, sitting on a mat in the courtyard. Golapi is washing utensils in another corner of the courtyard.

Padmabati: Now you have seen, dear, that my Lalu can do anything if he makes up his mind to do it. He chopped off that big tree all on his own!

Then she turns towards Lalu and says:

Padmabati: Lalu, my son, why don't you call on the Kabiraj-Moshai and try to secure a job at his place?

Golapi laughs with a short catch of breath and says—

Golapi: He is going to work! That would be the day! All he can do is – compose songs …

Lalu: Composing a song is much more difficult than planting a tree – do you get me, puny fish?

Padmabati: But that does not fill the tummy, son. There is a common saying – food before everything and then you may sing …

CUT

2 **M.L.S. to M.S.**
Camera outside Lalu's home. The Kabiraj is advancing on his horse, accompanied by Jadu, his footman. They stop in front of Lalu's cottage. The footman Jadu shouts –
Jadu: Lalu.
Then he advances towards their door.

CUT

3 **M.S.**
Camera in courtyard. Jadu enters through the door and says –
Jadu: Where are you people? Come, the Kabiraj is here . . .
A part of the horse standing still is seen in the background.

CUT

4 **M.S. (Same as Shot-1)**
Padmabati is startled; she hastily covers her head with her sari. Golapi washes her hands and stands up. Lalu advances from the kitchen. Padmabati speaks to Golapi in a whisper.
Padmabati: Did you see, daughter, God did hear my appeal. Go Lalu, go and talk about a job.
Padmabati gets to her feet as she says this.

CUT

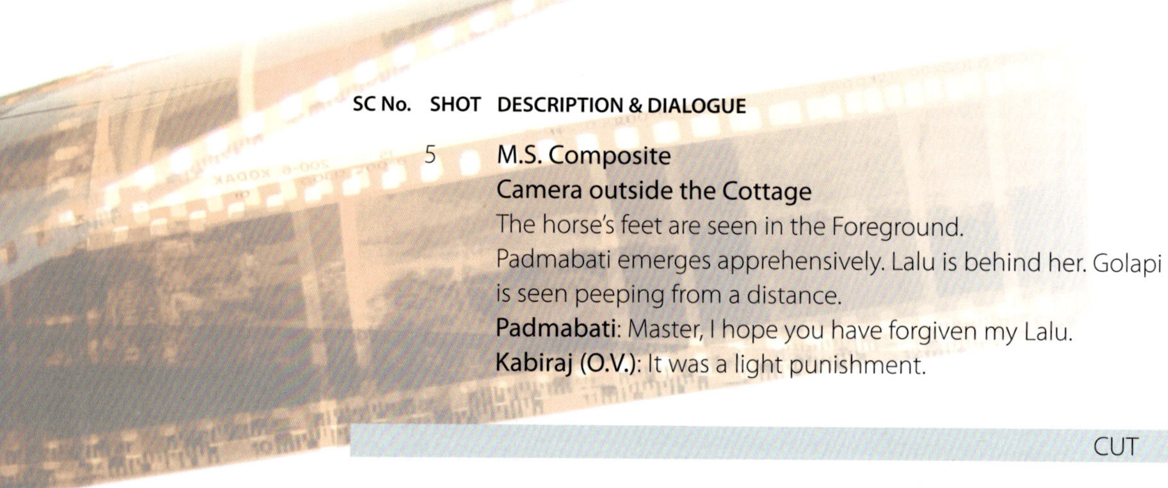

SC No.	SHOT	DESCRIPTION & DIALOGUE
	5	**M.S. Composite** **Camera outside the Cottage** The horse's feet are seen in the Foreground. Padmabati emerges apprehensively. Lalu is behind her. Golapi is seen peeping from a distance. **Padmabati**: Master, I hope you have forgiven my Lalu. **Kabiraj (O.V.)**: It was a light punishment.

CUT

	6	**M.C.S.** The Kabiraj is seen seated on the horse – from Padmabati's P.O.V. **Kabiraj**: But your son has done the job well. I am pleased and I have decided to give him a job.

CUT

	7	**M.S. Composite** Padmabati and Lalu are standing together. Golapi is at some distance. Padmabati joins her palms together to touch her temple in obeisance to the Kabiraj and says – **Padmabati**: You have been sent to us by God ...

CUT

	8	**M.C.S. (Same as Shot.-6)** **Kabiraj**: Now listen to me, Lalu. You will do your job and you may go on with your singing as well. Abdul is not in good health, on top of which he has become addicted to opium – Then he slaps the horse's back and says – **Kabiraj**: From now on you are going to look after Rani and I shall take care of you and your family ...

CUT

Behind the scenes (right and centre): Two outdoor stills, shot in Bolpur with the village Kabiraj and Lalon's mother Padmabati. These shots were finally dropped from the film

Between the shots: Director, actors, technicians and the horse Rani pose on the steps of the Kabiraj's mansion in Bolpur for a casual group photo

SC No. **SHOT** **DESCRIPTION & DIALOGUE**

9 **M.S. Composite (Same as Shot-7).**
Lalu's face brightens in pleasure. And Padmabati almost breaks down in tears.
Golapi draws closer with short steps and pulls down her sari to cover her face.
Kabiraj: You are very fond of Rani, aren't you?
Lalu smiles and nods his head. Behind the sari covering her face Golapi giggles and then runs back into the courtyard.

CUT

10 **M.C.S.**
Kabiraj: I shall be leaving on a trip with my family next Wednesday for taking a dip in the *Ganga. You will accompany me, look after Rani and also sing for me. You will be gaining three-fold in one trip — get cured of your horse-disease, go on a pilgrimage and earn some money as well.

CUT

11 **M.C.S. Composite**
On hearing this proposal Padmabati is seized with sudden alarm. In a moment her face becomes deathly pale.

CUT

12 **M.C.S.**
Kabiraj: We shall set off at dawn on the day after tomorrow.
He pulls on the horse's reins as he says this. The horse trots away.

CUT

13 **M.S. (Toppish)**
Pressing her hands to her mouth Padmabati rushes through the courtyard and enters the room. Lalu and Golapi appear in the Frame.
Sound of Padmabati's wailing is heard from the room. Golapi runs to the door. Lalu remains standing in a flabbergasted manner. Padmabati's lamentations are heard from inside the room.

* Ganga: River Ganges, held as sacred and worshipped by Hindus

SC No. SHOT DESCRIPTION & DIALOGUE

Padmabati: Why did you have to assign him this job, dear God? His father was lost when he went on such a pilgrimage. Oh God! Stop him, Golapi, do not let him go …

Lalu stands petrified in the middle of the courtyard. Padmabati's lamentations come floating from the room. Descending from the veranda Golapi moves towards Lalu with slow steps.

CUT

14 **M.C.S. (Composite)**

Golapi draws near Lalu with an apprehensive face. She fixes her eyes on Lalu's eyes. There are many questions in the eyes of the young girl.

The Camera tracks forward and goes close to Golapi.

DISSOLVE

SC No.	SHOT	DESCRIPTION & DIALOGUE
10	1	**Location: A village road.** **Time: Dawn** **M.L.S.** The eastern sky is brightening. But the sun has not risen yet. Kabiraj Krishnaprasanna Sen's party is moving forward after crossing a shallow swamp. The Kabiraj's wife and her maid Bina are travelling in a palanquin which is screened on all sides. Nishikanta, Raghab Datta and some other prominent persons of the village are travelling on foot. The Kabiraj is riding on his horse. Lalu is walking beside him. The footman Jadu and several servants carrying baggage are following them. After crossing the swamp the party now climbs onto a dyke.

CUT

SC No.	SHOT	DESCRIPTION & DIALOGUE
	2	**M.C.S.** The maid Bina's eyes are seen through a gap in the screen. Bina is looking at something with fascinated eyes.

CUT

3 **M.S. Travelling Shot**

From Bina's P.O.V. Lalu is seen walking. While walking Lalu looks around. As soon as he catches Bina's eyes Lalu breaks into a broad smile.

CUT

4 **M.C.S. (Same as Shot-2)**

Bina smiles briefly and then lowers her eyes shyly.

CUT

5 **L.S.**

The party is seen to proceed over the dyke, which is now grazed by the first light of dawn.

CUT

11 1 **Location: Shrine of Goddess Chandi in a village.**
Time: Night
M.S. Composite (on trolley)

Lights of several torch-fires are seen. In the Foreground rice is being cooked on two make-shift ovens. A servant is seen supervising the cooking. Sleeping arrangements for the Kabiraj and his wife have been made in an enclosed space – some distance away.

A song is heard in Lalu's voice on the Sound Track.

Lalu (Song):

Do not beat me any more, mother,
My body is writhing in pain.
I swear upon my heart, mother
Never shall I steal butter again.
For this little morsel of butter, mother
You have beaten me black and blue,
There is no kindness in your heart, mother
Now the whole world knows this to be true.
Do not beat me any more, mother . . .

Bina emerges from the enclosed space bearing a hookah prepared for the Kabiraj in her hand. **The Camera follows her.** She hands over the hookah to the Kabiraj. Two distinguished gentlemen from the village are sitting next to the Kabiraj. One of them is Raghab Datta and the other gentleman is Nishikanta Das. **The Camera tracks further and brings Lalu in the Frame.** Lalu is singing for the Kabiraj. After delivering the hookah to the Kabiraj, Bina flops down on the ground and goes on listening to Lalu's singing with a rapturous expression on her face.

Suddenly Giribala's loud voice is heard overlapping Lalu's song.

Giribala: Bina, you wretched girl, where have you perished?

On hearing Giribala's voice Bina quickly jumps to her feet. Lalu goes on singing.

CUT

SC No. SHOT DESCRIPTION & DIALOGUE

2 **M.C.S. to M.S. Composite**

The Camera follows Bina as she enters the temporarily enclosed space. Inside Giribala is seen fidgeting in the heat. On seeing Bina Giribala says –

Giribala: I am feeling stifled in this heat. Come, fan me for a while.

Bina quickly picks up a hand-fan and starts fanning her mistress. Giribala feels relieved after she is fanned for a while and says –

Giribala: Go and see if the cooking is finished. Tomorrow we have to wake up at the crack of dawn and take our dip in the Ganga.

Bina: Which task should I do first, mistress?

Giribala: Both.

Bina starts fanning her mistress even faster.

Giribala goes on grumbling to herself.

CUT

SC No.	SHOT	DESCRIPTION & DIALOGUE

3 **M.S. Composite (On trolley)**

Lalu is singing. The Kabiraj is listening to him with closed eyes and pulling at his hookah from time to time. His horse Rani is standing at some distance away. The footman Jadu and other servants are seen moving around in the Background. Lalu finishes his song.

4 The Kabiraj exclaims in praise.

Kabiraj: You are unique, Lalu.

After finishing the song Lalu remains sitting, holding his folded knees with both hands as tightly as he can.

Kabiraj: Now go and get your dinner and then go to sleep.

Lalu: I am not hungry, master—I feel very cold.

As the Kabiraj takes a close look at Lalu he realises that the lad is ill. He beckons Lalu. Lalu is shivering as he advances towards the Kabiraj.

The Camera tracks them composing in M.C.S. Composite.

The Kabiraj feels Lalu's pulse and says –

Kabiraj: This lad has high fever. Jadu, go and get a thick sheet and my medicine box …

CUT

12 1 **Location: Shrine of Goddess Chandi in village.**

Time: Midnight.

M.S.

The enclosed space where the Kabiraj and Giribala are sleeping can be seen. The dim light of a small oil-lamp is flickering in the enclosed space. The lamp is about to go off. The loud snoring of the Kabiraj and his wife is heard, somewhat like a rhythmic question and answer session.

CUT

2 **M.S. (low angle)**

Rani, the Kabiraj's horse seems to be in a restless state and is unable to stand still. Abruptly an inarticulate sound emerges from his mouth.

CUT

SC No. **SHOT** **DESCRIPTION & DIALOGUE**

3 **M.C.S. Composite**

Lalu has been laid under a shed of bulrush, his body wrapped with a sheet. An oil-lamp burns near his head.

Bina is mopping his fevered forehead with a torn piece of cloth soaked in water. Bina asks in a soft whisper –

Bina: Are you in a lot of pain? You haven't eaten anything.
Would you like to eat a little puffed rice with sugar-drops?

Lalu is lying unconscious. He does not reply. His fever is so high that the cloth dries very fast. Bina soaks it in water again and places it on his forehead.

CUT

13 1 **Location: Shrine of Goddess Chandi in village**
Time: Morning
M.C.S.
Lalu is lying unconscious. His entire face and throat are covered by red blisters. A few flies are buzzing over his eyes. The Kabiraj's Off voice overlaps.
Kabiraj: It is small pox.

CUT

2 Raghab Datta advances and says –
Raghab Datta: He is totally unconscious.

CUT

3 The Kabiraj is leaning over to examine Lalu.
Raghab Datta and Nishikanta Das are standing a little away. Giribala and Bina draw near them, their heads covered with their saris. The footman Jadu is also seen in the background.
Kabiraj: There is nothing to be done. It is an affliction bestowed by the Divine Mother, beyond the scope of cure by medical science . . .

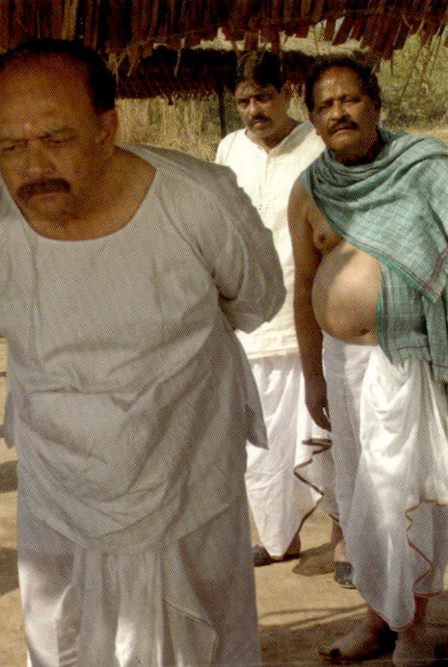

Giribala: It is so sad… the poor boy travelled all this distance, but was still denied the opportunity of taking a dip in the holy Ganga. What do you suggest, * Purohit Moshai?

CUT

4 M.C.S.

Purohit: Do what you think best. After all we have to think of his after-life.

CUT

5 **Kabiraj**: You people better go and finish your bath. Jadu, ask the bearers to take the mistress for her bath. We'll go after attending to this matter.

CUT

* Purohit : A priest

6 **M.C.S.**
Bina bursts into tears.
Giribala: Come, Bina …

CUT

7 **M.S. Composite (Shrine of Goddess Chandi in Village)**
The Kabiraj is sitting in the courtyard of the temple, smoking his hookah with a grave face. Raghab Datta, Nishikanta Das and the footman Jadu are with him. Raghab Datta breaks the silence.

Raghab Datta: Kabiraj Moshai, instead of burning him, can't we float him in the Ganga … may be the poor fellow could then gain a little piety …

Kabiraj: Listen, Raghab, how can he gain piety when he has no life? Any way, since you have mentioned it, let us do as you say …

Suddenly the Kabiraj seems to come to his senses.

Kabiraj: But who is going to touch him? This is a highly contagious disease!

Jadu scratches his head and says –

Jadu: Master, may I make a suggestion –

The Kabiraj looks at Jadu.

Jadu: The urchins who beg at the river-bank … may be something can be arranged by paying them a little money …

Kabiraj: Do it. Complete his last rites and then float him in the Ganga … I shall bear whatever expenses are incurred.

Nishikanta Das: If we spend money we can even get tiger's milk if we want it. This is nothing …
Come Jadu.

Kabiraj casts a single glance at Nishikanta and then starts pulling at his hookah. The others go out.

CUT

8 **MCS**

Rani is standing next to the shed of bulrushes, where Lalu's body is lying. She lets off a sharp neigh.

CUT

SC No.	SHOT	DESCRIPTION & DIALOGUE
14	1	Location: A solitary place by the Ganga Time: Morning M.S. to M.L.S (Camera at low level) Lalu has been laid on a raft made of banana stalks. His body is covered by a sheet. Nets woven with threads are hung all around, tied to bamboo twigs fixed to four corners of the raft. Incense sticks have been pegged into the raft. A few half-naked urchins drag the raft to the middle of the river.
		CUT
	2	M.L.S. (Long focus lens) The banana stalk-raft carrying Lalu is floating on the river in a swaying movement.
		DISSOLVE
	3	(Like Title Shot) (Long focus lens) The raft goes on floating in dim light—similar to the fading light of dusk in the Title shot.

SC No.	SHOT	DESCRIPTION & DIALOGUE
		The sound of a single-stringed lute and a song in Lalon's adult voice, comes floating in the Background. **Lalon (Song)**: *Whiling away my time till the very last day . . .*
		CUT
15	1	**Location: House Boat** **Time: Diffused Light** **M.S. to M.C.S. (on trolley)** Old Lalon Fakir is singing while playing on a single-stringed lute. **As the song is in progress the Camera tracks and reaches his MCS**. *My childhood was spent in fun and game,* *My youth was tainted with disgrace and shame,* *Death came at old age, calling me by name* *And thus to the clutches of eternity I fell prey* *– whiling away my time till the very last day . . .*
	2	Jyotirindra's Off Voice is heard. **Jyotirindra**: Excellent!
		CUT

SC No.	SHOT	DESCRIPTION & DIALOGUE
	3	**M.S. to C.S.** Jyotirindranath's profile. A sketch-book is laid on an easel before him. Jyotirindranath draws the last line on the sketch and is about to write his name.
		CUT
	4	**Camera on the easel.** Jyotirindranath's hand writes beside the sketch – *Lalon Fakir* *On Silaidaha Boat* *– Jyotirindranath Tagore* *1889.*
		CUT
	5	**M.S. Composite** In the foreground writing pad, pen, books and other odds and bits are lying on a table. Lalon's unfinished sketch is displayed on the easel. Jyotirindranath picks up a tin of cigarettes from the table and extends it towards Lalon. **Jyotirindranath**: Fakir sahib … **Lalon**: What is this? **Jyotirindranath**: Cigarette – you may call it the Englishman's *bidi*. Try it, you will enjoy it … Lalon takes a cigarette and rolls it around in his hand, looking at it closely. **Lalon**: This looks quite nice, very neat. Jyotirindranath lights up his own cigarette and then extends the lighted match towards Lalon. Lalon lights up his cigarette and pulls at it with a lot of relish. **Jyotirindranath**: Come, let us go back to the bungalow before it gets dark. We can have our conversation there. **Lalon**: Very well.
		CUT

Do not beat me any more, mother,
My body is writhing in pain.
I swear upon my heart, mother
Never shall I steal butter again.
For this little morsel of butter, mother
You have beaten me black and blue,
There is no kindness in your heart, mother
Now the whole world knows this to be true.
Do not beat me any more, mother ....

Aar amare marish ne ma
Boli ma tor choron dhorey noni churi aar korbo na
Nonir jonyo aaj amarey
Marli go ma bendhey dhorey
Doya nai ma tor antarey
Shwalpetey gelo jana
Aar amarey marish ne ma

Scene 11; Shot 12

16 1 **Location: A strip of sandy land by the river-bank**
Time: Dusk is approaching
M.L.S.

In the Foreground the houseboat is seen standing by the river-bank. Old Lalon and Jyotirindranath enter the Frame. Lalon walks with the help of his stick. Jyotirindranath walks with him, followed by the servants.

CUT

2 **M.S. (On Trolley) Reverse Angle**
The houseboat is in the Background. Lalon and Jyotirindranath are advancing.
Jyotirindranath: Fakir sahib, do you believe in rebirth?
Lalon: The mortal life's all that it is, Babu Moshai. There is a void before and a void after it. And for this hapless one it's been two births in one.

CUT

SC No.	SHOT	DESCRIPTION & DIALOGUE
17	1	**Location: An old tree and the stump of a palm tree laid on the bank of river Ganga** **Time: Morning** **M.S.to M.L.S. Camera on Crane** The wide river is in the Frame. A young boy, swimming in the river, enters the Frame. **The Camera pans and the Crane is raised up**. A dead, dry tree lies uprooted on the river. The boy grabs a dried branch and becomes still.
		CUT
	2	**M.S.** Lalu's body lies on the raft.
		CUT
	3	**M.C.S.** The boy catches sight of something and shrinks in fear. Unconsciously, a few words slip out from his mouth— **Boy**: Hai, Allah!
		CUT
	4	**M.L.S. (Toppish) the boy's P.O.V.** A raft made of banana stalks is caught in the roots of the dead tree. The net has slipped down, but a corpse is clearly discernible through it. Suddenly, a groaning sound is heard.
		CUT
	5	**M.L.S. Composite On Crane (Toppish)** In the Foreground three women are bathing by the river-bank. The young boy swims very fast from the root of the dead tree and then heaves himself up on the bank in a single leap. He then addresses the women—

Boy: Oh, foster-mother, there is a dead man lying there – and he is making some strange noises too … Allah …
And he runs away.

CUT

6 **M.S. Composite**
Of the three women one is aged about thirty, the other two are a little younger. The name of the older woman is Rabeya, the other two are Khadija and Fatema.
Rabeya: Come, let us go and see …
The other two women have paled in fear.
Fatema: Let us get away from here — who knows what is lying there …
Rabeya: Come on, you scared cat —
Rabeya starts moving towards the dead tree as she says this.
Khadija: Please do not go there, aunt Rabeya…
Without bothering to reply, Rabeya advances towards the dead tree. **The Camera follows her.**

CUT

SC No.	SHOT	DESCRIPTION & DIALOGUE
	7	**M.S. Composite (Toppish)** At one end of the Frame the raft of banana stalks is stuck in the root of the dead tree. The net has got wrapped all round the dead body. Rabeya wades through chest-high water to enter the Frame. Inarticulate groaning sounds are emerging from the mouth of the corpse from time to time. Rabeya removes the net very carefully. Inflamed small pox sores are seen all over the body; they have become pale through prolonged exposure to water. Rabeya calls out in a loud voice – **Rabeya**: Oh, Khadija, oh Fatema, come here. It's neither a ghost, nor a demon. It is a living person …
		CUT
18	1	**Location: Rabeya's hut** **Time: Morning** **Fixed Frame** Lalu is lying on a mat. His head and a portion of the chest is visible. There are inflamed sores on his head and body. His eyes are closed. His body is coated with mud and clay.
		MIX
	2	Lalu is lying in the same manner. There is no mud or clay on his body, indicating that he has been cleaned up.
		MIX
	3	The sores on the face and body are healed. The blisters have dried up and turned to scabs. A woman's hand lightly runs a small branch of neem leaves on his body and then exits the Frame.
		MIX

Crossing the river: Working stills from the film. Director Goutam Ghose and Prosenjit Chattopadhyay with the crew

4 The scabs have dropped off from the body.
Now there are deep pock-marks on the face and on the rest of the body.
Rabeya enters bringing milk in a brass cup.
Dipping a cotton wick in the milk she puts milk drop by drop into Lalu's mouth.
The sound of drawing a weaver's shuttle floats in – Off Frame.

CUT

5 **M.S.**
Kalimuddin, Rabeya's husband, is weaving on a loom and grumbling.
Kalimuddin: Did you burn the scabs properly?
Rabeya does not reply. Still weaving on his loom, Kalimuddin speaks again –
Kalimuddin: She had to drag home a small-pox patient from somewhere and now she says that he has been sent by Allah.

CUT

6 **M.S.**
As she walks from the cow-shed across the courtyard with the brass cup in her hand, Rabeya says –
Rabeya: Yes, it is Allah who has sent him! You did not give me any . . .

CUT

7 **M.C.S.**

Abruptly Kalimuddin stops the weaver's shuttle and says –

Kalimuddin: People in the neighbourhood are saying that a murrain is bound to break in. This is a highly contagious disease.

CUT

8 **M.S. Composite on Trolley**

Rabeya: Do I pay tax to those people for living here? I have worked as a nurse for all these years – this disease is nothing new to me.

Rabeya draws near the weaver's workshop as she says this.

Rabeya: The lad has not spoken a word till now. You could have at least prayed for his recovery, but no, you had to scare me about murrains. You are really a heartless man!

Instead of continuing with the argument Kalimuddin resumes working at his loom. The rattling noise of the weaver's shuttle is heard. Rabeya walks back towards the cowshed.

CUT

9 **C.S.**

Very slowly Lalu tries to open his eyes. One eye is closed, but his spirit has been restored.

CUT

SC No.	SHOT	DESCRIPTION & DIALOGUE

10 **M.C.S.**
The indistinct face of a woman appears in the Frame. Rabeya stoops down a little as she advances towards Lalu.

CUT

11 **M.C.S. (Composite)**
Lalu is in Preference. A strange sound emerges from his mouth
Lalu: M .. aa .. . . .
Tears of joy appear in Rabeya's eyes.
Rabeya: What is you name, son?
Lalu goes on looking blankly at her.
Rabeya: Where is you home, son, can you remember anything?
Lalu shakes his head slightly.

CUT

12 Lalu can remember nothing. Only countless waves float before his eyes.

CUT

13 **C.S.**
Lalu speaks in a feeble voice.
Lalu: I am hungry . . .

CUT

14 **M.C.S.**
Rice is being cooked in an earthen pot. Water from the boiling rice starts overflowing from the pot.
Rabeya's hand shifts the earthen plate from the top of the pot to provide a little opening.
The Camera is tilted up to focus on Rabeya's face.

CUT

15 **M.C.S.**
Kalimuddin is sitting on a veranda near the kitchen and smoking from a hookah.

SC No.	SHOT	DESCRIPTION & DIALOGUE
		Kalimuddin: He cannot remember his name or address. How did you know that he does not belong to our religion?
		CUT
16		**M.C.S.** **Rabeya**: But didn't I change his clothes? Rabeya falls silent after saying this.
		CUT
	17	**M.C.S.** Kalimuddin is at first confused on hearing Rabeya's statement. Then he realises that she has hinted about circumcision. Unconsciously, two words emerge from his mouth **Kalimuddin**: Hai, Allah!
		CUT
	18	**M.C.S.** **Rabeya**: Whatever may be his caste or religion, isn't it a sin to deny food to a sick man when he is hungry?
		CUT
	19	**C.S. to M.C.S. (On trolley)** Lalu's Profile as he is in a half-reclined position. Rabeya's hand is seen feeding soft rice to Lalu. **The Camera backs to show Rabeya.** She is feeding soft rice to Lalu from a brass plate. On the Sound track the voice of old Lalon is heard, breaking into a few lines of a song – **Lalon (Song):** *When you become a fakir, you mad man,* *How will you make your plans?* *Can you not see Hindus and Muslims* *are split up as two clans …*
		CUT

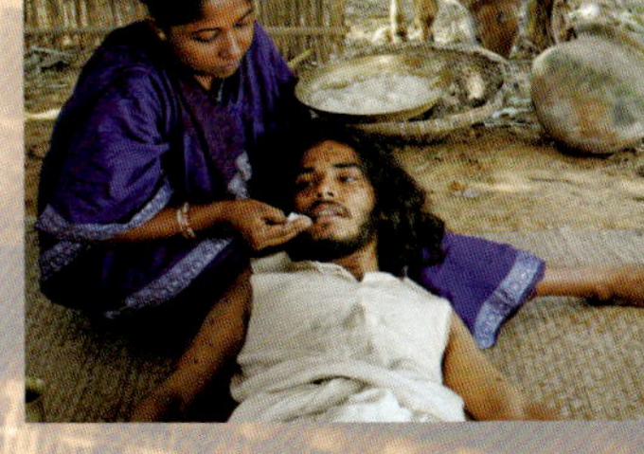

Vignettes from the shooting zone. Director Goutam Ghose and his leading man Prosenjit Chattopadhyay on location

SC No.	SHOT	DESCRIPTION & DIALOGUE
19	1	**Location: Bungalow in Silaidaha** **Time: Evening** **M.C.S. (on trolley)** Jyotirindranath's Profile. He is listening to Lalon's singing. An ornamental lamp has been lit and kept on the table. **The Camera tracks to focus on old Lalon.** Lalon finishes his song and smiles briefly.
	2	**Lalon**: In this world there are only two castes – man and woman … the rest are all human misdoings … This is what my Guru had taught me … Siraj Sain … the light of my life … Lalon lifts his right hand to his forehead as he says this. Siraj Sain's song is heard on Sound Track – *Is the 'jol' above 'pani' or the 'pani' above 'jol' …* O/L

CUT

20	1	**Location: A musical function at Jolagram.** **Time: Night** **M.S. low angle (wide angle lens)** Siraj Sain is singing and dancing at the function. He carries a stringed instrument in his hand. Musicians and a few other men are sitting on either side of Siraj Sain, the rest are fakir singers. **Siraj Sain**: *Is the 'jol' above 'pani'* **(Song)** *or the 'pani' above 'jol' …* **Chorus**: *Tell me, oh Khuda,* **(Song)** *tell me, oh lord …* **Siraj Sain**: *Is Kali above Ali* **(Song)** *or Ali above Kali …* **Chorus**: *Tell me, oh Khuda,* *tell me, oh lord ….*

CUT

*'Jol' and 'Pani': Words used in Bengali by Hindus and Muslims respectively to mean 'water'

SC No.	SHOT	DESCRIPTION & DIALOGUE

Behind the scene: Prosenjit Chattopadhyay in old Lalon's costume and make up, putting on the last touches for the houseboat scene

2 **M.L.S.to M.S.**

Men and women of different ages from the village are sitting and listening to the song.

The Camera is lowered down. In the Foreground Lalu too is seen sitting with Rabeya and listening.

Siraj Sain: *The earth is at the bottom*
(Song) *and above floats the sky*
or are they both set up
equally high ...
Chorus: *Tell me, oh Khuda,*
tell me, oh lord ...

CUT

3 **M.S. to C.S. (Fixed Camera)**

While singing Siraj Sain moves back and again comes forward. At the end of the Shot he jumps up in the air and his face goes out of the Frame.

Siraj Sain: *In a cemetery a Hindu*
(Song) *is set on fire*
and in a graveyard a Mian
is buried in earth ...
Tell me which is higher
Tell me what each is worth ...

CUT

4 **M.L.S. Composite (Toppish)**

Audience in the Foreground. The stage for the musical function is at the rear.

Chorus: *Tell me, oh Khuda,*
tell me, oh lord ...
Siraj Sain: *Is the jol above pani*
(Song) *or the pani above jol ...*
Chorus: *Tell me, oh Khuda,*
tell me, oh lord ...

CUT

SC No.	SHOT	DESCRIPTION & DIALOGUE
21	1	**Location: Courtyard in Rabeya's cottage.** **Time: Night** **M.C.S. to M.S. (on trolley)** Animated discussions between Siraj Sain and the local fakirs and minstrels are in progress. Kalimuddin has invited a few important persons from the neighbourhood. The Shot begins with a fakir pulling at the bowl of a hookah containing opium. Then he extends the bowl towards Siraj Sain. **The Camera tracks to Compose everyone.** Siraj Sain takes a long pull from the bowl and then extends it towards another person. **Siraj Sain**: Now tell me, Kalimuddin …
		CUT
	2	**M.C.S.** **Kalimuddin**: These gentlemen have some questions for fakir Siraj Sain …
		CUT
	3	**M.C.S.** **Siraj Sain**: Fakir – pooh! Do I have any knowledge or wisdom? I have put on this ascetic's garb, grown a long beard, so people treat me with a little fear and respect and feed me when I call on them – that's all!
		CUT
	4	The invitees remain silent. **Kalimuddin**: Why are you keeping quiet? Ask him what you want. He is my first cousin. He comes here off and on … **One guest**: Anwar Mian, you better ask him … **Anwar**: Sain-ji, our Maulavi sahib says that the Koran of ten chapters preached by the Fakirs is not the true Islamic Koran … what is your view?
		CUT

SC No.	SHOT	DESCRIPTION & DIALOGUE

5 **M.S. (Rabeya's kitchen)**

Rabeya is cooking kedgeree in a large cauldron.

She takes out a little kedgeree with a ladle, feels it with her fingers to see if the rice has softened after boiling. Lalu stands next to her with a blank expression on his face.

Rabeya: Yes, the job is done. Come, let us now go and listen to Sain-ji …

Siraj Sain (O.V.): Why would those who have mastered the secret theory of ten chapters listen to the dictates of an instructor who preaches thirty chapters? The compilation of ten chapters is known as Dil-Koran or the heart of Islam.

CUT

6 **M.C.S. (Composite) Toppish**

A group is sitting before Siraj Sain. Rabeya enters the Frame with Lalu.

Rabeya: The food is ready. You may eat now if you wish …

She makes Lalu sit down close to Siraj Sain's feet and then addresses Lalu.

Rabeya: Make your obeisance …

CUT

7 **M.C.S. Composite**

Siraj Sain, Rabeya and Lalu.

Rabeya: This is my son – please bless him … I picked him up from the river bank. He has been sent to me by Allah …

Siraj Sain: I know – you have done a very pious act by saving him, Rabeya, … you have secured your passage for the next world …

CUT

8 **Rabeya**: He is a most unfortunate lad. He has no recollection of his name or address …

Lalu looks on blankly.

Siraj Sain: I think I have seen him somewhere … not in the river … on land …

SC No.	SHOT	DESCRIPTION & DIALOGUE
		Rabeya is startled on hearing what Siraj Sain says. Siraj Sain leans forward a little to look closely at Lalu. **The Camera tracks and goes close to Lalu.**
		CUT
22	1	**Location: The bank of Ganga** **Time: Dawn** **M.L.S. to M.S. (on Trolley)** The Foreground of a tree. The river Ganga flows behind. A song is heard in Lalu's voice Off Frame. **The Camera tracks Lalu and brings him in Frame.** Lalu sits by the river-bank and sings – some long-lost song, like a lingering memory of a previous life. **Lalu (Song):** *Just on two wheels my car still runs its course* *On it Sain, you have built a house of three floors.*
		CUT

SC No. SHOT DESCRIPTION & DIALOGUE

2 **M.S. to M.C.S.**

Lalu is singing as he sits by the river bank.

Lalu (Song):

Oh Sain, my respected Guru, my lord
and master
please tell me where I can dump this
enormous monster …

From the Background of the Frame Siraj Sain enters the Frame and comes walking towards Lalu. Then he sits down beside Lalu who stops singing. He seems to be lost in some dreamland.

The Camera tracks to reach their M.C.S.

Siraj Sain places a hand on Lalu's shoulder and says –

3 **M.S. Composite On Trolley**

Siraj Sain: Now you have got your memory back! What more can you remember?

Abruptly Siraj Sain shakes up Lalu with a lot of force and enquires –

Siraj Sain: What is your name … can you remember?

Words emerge inarticulately from Lalu's mouth.

Lalu: Lalon Chandra Kar.

Siraj Sain embraces him in joy and says –

Siraj Sain: Son, there is a time when one has to keep oneself under cover and then a time comes when one has to expose oneself. And listen Lalon, whatever is lost is no longer yours.

Lalon: What should I do? Where would I go?

Siraj Sain: Anywhere you wish … is there any dearth of space in this wide world?

But first and foremost you have to find out who you are. Remember, son, among all that you have to find out the most important thing is to find yourself.

Lalon: Please tell me how I can do it.

SC No. SHOT DESCRIPTION & DIALOGUE

Siraj Sain: Of course, I will tell you. I will tell you everything that I know—I will give you all that I have . . .
Siraj Sain's face becomes bright –
Siraj Sain: Do you know what I possess? A palace of winds! A town of mirrors! A hill of crystals! A strange, exquisite bird! Do you want to have them?
Lalon: Yes, I do, Sainji.

CUT

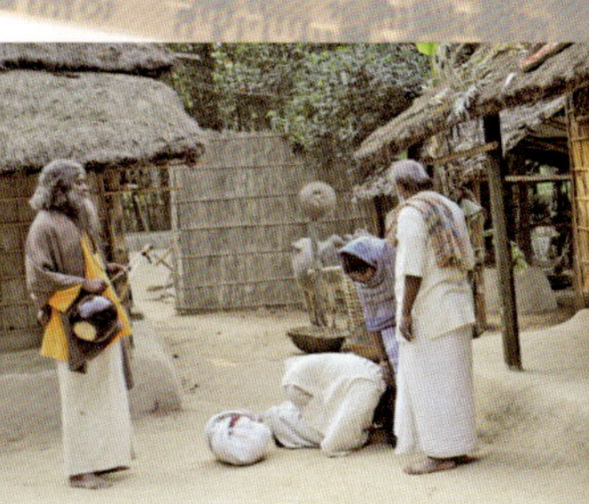

23 1 **Location: Rabeya's home**
Time: Late evening
M.S. to M.L.S. (Camera on Crane trolley)
The Shot is launched at a slightly Toppish position. Vacant courtyard. Siraj Sain enters the Frame and walks down to stand in a corner. Rabeya enters the Frame holding Lalon's arm.
A sound of suppressed sobbing is heard. Kalimuddin is behind them.
They come and stand in the middle of the courtyard. Lalon touches the feet of Rabeya and Kalimuddin in obeisance. Siraj Sain, standing still and composed, says –
Siraj Sain: Come, bless your son from the bottom of your heart. He is now going to row his boat in an ocean of blissful ecstasy.
Siraj Sain starts walking. Lalon follows him, carrying a small bundle on his shoulder.

CUT

2 **M.L.S. (Marshy area) On Crane**
In the fading light of dusk a strip of land seems to have merged with the water. In the distance the river-water has been tinged with the colour of twilight. Siraj Sain and Lalon enter the Frame and fade away in the distance.

CUT

Just on two wheels my car still runs its course,
On it *Sain, you have built a house of three floors;
...
Oh, Sain, my respected Guru, my lord and master,
Please tell me where I can dump this enormous monster;

Amar mattor duikhan chaka aar ekkhan gari
Tar upor banaichho sain teen mohola bari
...
Sain amaar porom pujji guru goshain
Bol barir bojha garir thikey kotha namai

Scene 7; Shot 1

SC No.	SHOT	DESCRIPTION & DIALOGUE
	3	**M.S.** Rabeya is sobbing with her head against a post in the veranda. Kalimuddin stands beside her; his eyes are glistening with tears. Kalimuddin hurries into the room. **The Camera holds Rabeya.** The sound of drawing a weaver's shuttle starts emerging from the room. Its regular tapping sound seems to mingle with the sound of Rabeya's sobbing like a background music. The rumble of clouds is heard on the Sound Track.

CUT

SC No.	SHOT	DESCRIPTION & DIALOGUE

24 1 **Location: The bungalow at Silaidaha**

Time: Night

A dark room. Only a single red lamp burns in one corner. A lamp placed in the veranda had gone out, but has been re-lit. It is raining.

A servant enters bearing another lamp.

Jyotirindranath and Lalon are seen in a sudden flash of lightning. The sketch-book is lying on the easel.

The servant advances to light up a lamp kept on the writing table.

Jyotirindranath: I am filled with regret whenever I think that I had not heard about a great devotee like Siraj Sain …

Lalon: But he is alive in the midst of all of us.

The table-lamp has been lit.

CUT

2 Lalon starts humming a song —

Lalon (Song):

Without a destination no boat can row,
Empty formlessness no mind can know,
Lalon wanders aimlessly to and fro,
He is set to have the intangible in tow,
And yet, the barjakh's help he has chosen to forego …

CUT

3 **M.C.S.**

With the singing of the last line there is overlapping on Jyotirindranath.

Jyotirindranath: What is the meaning of 'barjakh'?

CUT

4 **M.S. to M.C.S.**

Lalon: 'Barjakh' means a guru or preceptor … he is the boatman …

Then he points at himself and says –

Lalon: And a devotee's body is a boat. The waves on the river symbolise desires. Without a Guru a boat is powerless to move – the boatman is Alek Sain … he is the Guru, the master – the one and only person the mind and soul crave for; he is the one we madly search for all the time …

CUT

5 **M.C.S.**

Jyotirindranath: Does that mean to search for oneself? To search for one's inner soul?

CUT

6 **M.C.S.**

Lalon: To search for oneself means searching someone else– searching for someone else means searching for everyone and searching for everyone means searching for God …

CUT

7 **M.C.S.**

Jyotirindranath: I have a feeling that the theory of pantheism – that He exists in everything – is mentioned in the Upanishads. *Everything in this world is enveloped by Him.*

CUT

Where will I find the one;
Whom my heart craves in bitter pain ...
Having lost him, here and there I run
Searching everywhere, but all in vain ...

Ami kothaye paabo taarey
Amar moner manush jerey
Haraye shei manushey taar uddeshey
Desh bideshey berai ghurey

Scene 67; Shot 1

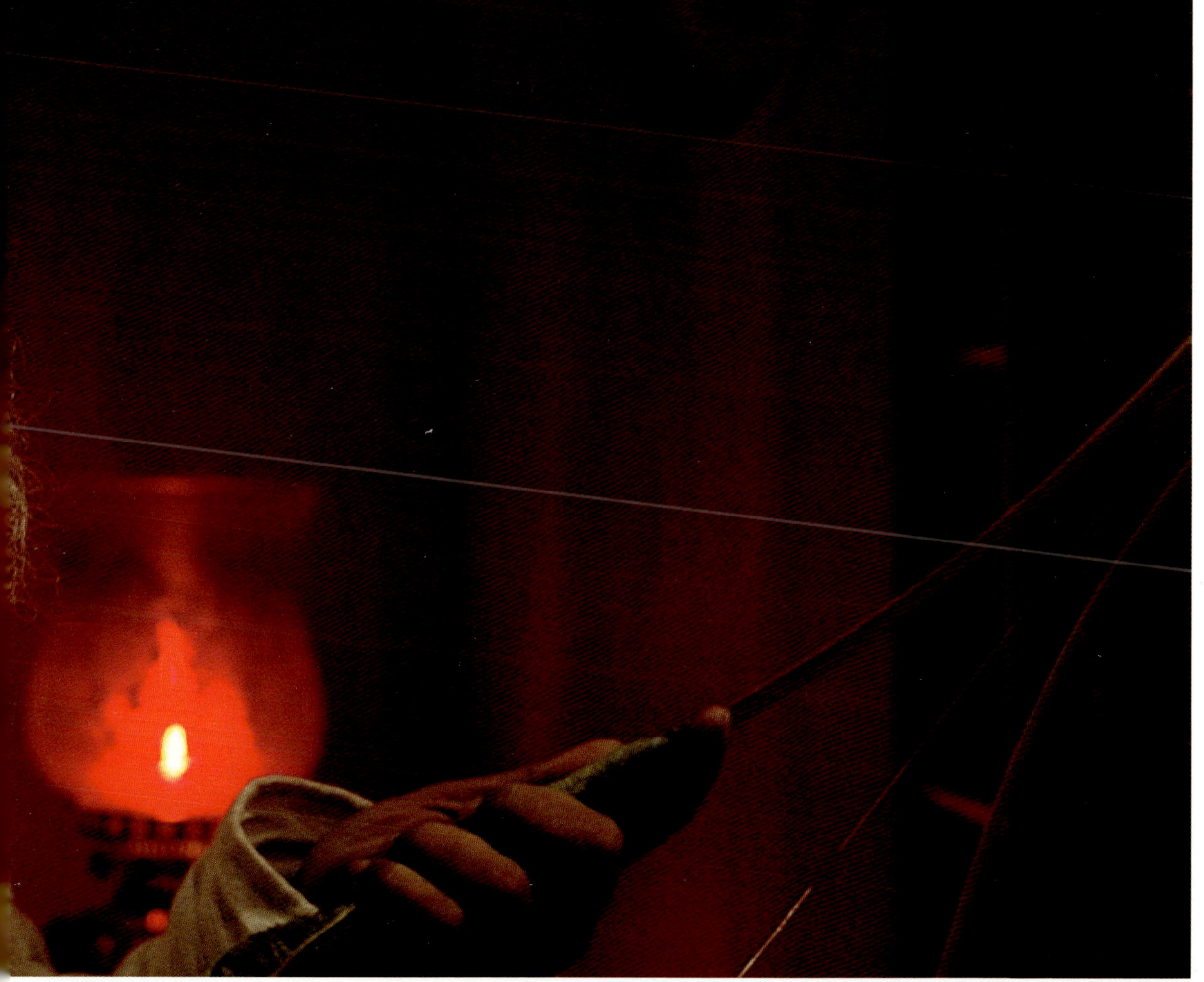

8 **M.C.S.**

Lalon: I am an illiterate man, I can't understand all those high-sounding words. But I do know that searching for the one whom the heart craves is not the same as searching for God, – it is a search for something much, much greater …

CUT

9 **M.C.S.**

Jyotirindranath: I am having a little difficulty in understanding your complex theory. Sometimes I feel that I have grasped the matter, but the next moment you seem to have shifted from your earlier stand …

CUT

10 **M.S. Composite**

Jyotirindranath is in the Foreground, Lalon is behind him. While talking Lalon gets to his feet and advances towards Jyotirindranath –

Lalon: Searching for the man whom the heart craves is a very complicated task, Babu Moshai. Here you see him for a second, but the next moment he is lost!

My Guru has winded me up like a toy and left me in such a state that I have been going round and round all my life. So many years of my life have been exhausted swinging like this!

CUT

SC No.	SHOT	DESCRIPTION & DIALOGUE
25	1	Location: Beside a marsh (Thick mist) Time: Dawn M.L.S. to M.C.S. (On Crane) There is thick mist. A figure in saffron is advancing from a distance. A cloth bag hangs from the person's shoulder. The saffron robe he is wearing has many patches and has become dirty through long travel on foot. His long hair is loose and he wears a band on his forehead. His beard is long and unkempt. Small pox scars are distinctly visible on his sun-burnt coppery face. The person can now be recognised. He is young Lalon Fakir. He comes and sits down under a tree.

CUT

2 **M.S.**

Sitting under the tree Lalon looks straight ahead.

CUT

3 **M.S.**

Siraj Sain is seen sitting under a tree imagined by Lalon. A light mist is seen to move away from his face. Siraj Sain seems to be saying –

Siraj Sain: From now onwards you are a minstrel and a fakir, you have renounced all worldly ties, you no longer have a family, you are not bound by any scruples of previous lives and you have no prejudices. You cannot become a minstrel if you retain even the slightest attachment to your past. Do you understand me, son?

Siraj Sain is enveloped by mist.

CUT

4 **M.L.S. (Toppish)**

Lalon is sitting under the tree. Moving the hand-bag a little away, he lays his head on it and lies down. The voice of old Lalon is heard.

Lalon (V.O.) : I had disobeyed the instructions of my Guru only once … After all I am a human being … when many years had passed I had an urge to see my mother… meet my wife … the village where I spent my childhood had called me.

CUT

A puny fish jumped up from the pond too soon
At an odd hour on a Saturday afternoon …
So ripples after ripples rose upon the water-bed.
And to the woods, eluding me, my mind's bird fled.
Ripples after ripples made the water-bed sway.
What trick did my mind's bird play as it flew away?

Puna maachhey laaph marichhey pukurey
Shonibaarer baar belatey dukurey
Tai dheuer porey dheu uthilo joley
Tai amar moner pakhi boney palaye ki chholey
Dheuer porey dheu uthilo joley
Moner pakhi boney palaye ki kausholey …

Scene 8; Shot 6

26 1 **Location: Lalu's village (The bank of a village-pond)**
Time: Morning.
M.S. to M.C.S.
Golapi is seen rising from the pond, carrying a brass pitcher filled with water on her waist. Much older now, she wears a widow's traditional dress and her hair is cut very short. As she climbs up on the bank and goes to M.C.S. position, her eyes fall on a fakir. Golapi pulls down the sari on her head.
A male voice is heard from Off.
Lalon (O.V.): Somehow, you look familiar … what is your name, woman?
Golapi is startled to hear the voice of a strange man.
Then she says –
Golapi: This humble maid is known as Golapi …

CUT

2 Lalon in the garb of a minstrel is seen from Golapi's P.O.V. It is almost impossible for Golapi to recognise Lalon. Assuming that he is a minstrel-fakir, Golapi keeps the pitcher on the ground and is about to make her obeisance to him. Lalon keeps looking steadily at Golapi.

CUT

3 **M.C.S.** (Low Level)
Golapi touches Lalon's feet in *pranam* and then says –

Golapi: Bless me, now …
Lalon extends his bag to her seeking alms.

CUT

4 **M.S. Composite**
Golapi lifts the pitcher to her waist and says –
Golapi: What alms shall I give you, Gosainji, we are in worse straits than beggars. But do come to our humble home, let it be blessed by your visit … I will give you whatever we have …
Lalon: I am begging for my youth … will you give it back to me?
Lalon (Song):
A puny fish jumped up from the pond too soon
At some odd hour on a Saturday afternoon …

CUT

5 Golapi is startled. She tries to hide her face with her two hands. Without her knowledge the pitcher starts rolling down towards the pond, spilling and spraying water all the way.

CUT

6 Golapi runs in the direction of the village without stopping. Lalon keeps standing still at the same spot.

CUT

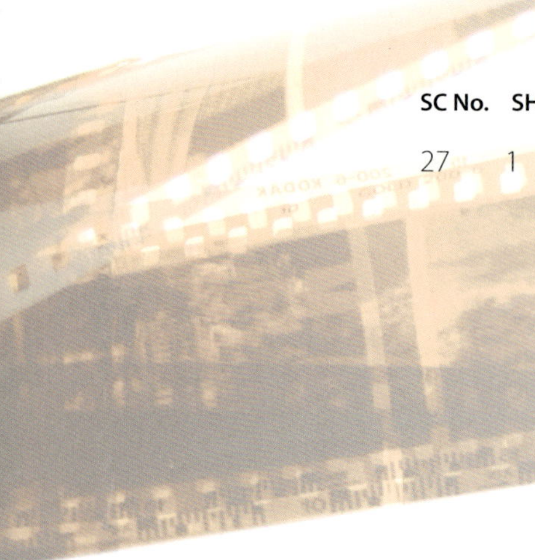

SC No. SHOT DESCRIPTION & DIALOGUE

27 1 **Location: Lalu's cottage**
Time: Morning
M.C.S. to C.S. (On trolley)

In the Foreground a single post of the veranda is in Sharp Focus. Lalon and Padmabati are Out of Focus in the Background. Padmabati is much older.

From Out of Focus Padmabati advances towards the post. Her face shows extreme concern. It seems as if she is about to swoon.

Padmabati is muttering –

Padmabati: What a strange story you have told me, Lalu. I cannot believe it ...

Lalon: Mother ...

Padmabati holds on to the post and sits down on the floor. Lalon advances from Out of Focus and puts his arms around his mother.

Padmabati goes on speaking in a daze.

Padmabati: Do not touch me, please do not touch me ... you have become an outcaste ... you have eaten at the hands of infidels ... dear God, why did this have to happen to me !

As she says this she starts wailing and striking her head against the post. **Camera tracks and reaches Golapi at the other end of the veranda**. Golapi grips the edge of the sari covering her head between her teeth and breaks into sobs.

SC No.	SHOT	DESCRIPTION & DIALOGUE
	2	**M.S. (Toppish)** Circles are forming on the surface of the pond surrounded by palm trees.
28	1	**Location: The courtyard of Lalu's cottage.** **Time: Afternoon.** The courtyard and the outer area of the cottage are thronged by people from the village. A few half-naked children are also seen in the crowd.
		MIX
	2	**C.S. (Travelling Shot)** An important man from the village advances with inquisitive eyes. **The Camera is backing.** The man stops after advancing a few steps. Staring at the lens, i.e. at Lalu for a while he shakes his head to indicate 'no'.
		MIX
	3	An old woman is seen to advance in a similar way. She too shakes her head to indicate 'no'.
		MIX

SC No.	SHOT	DESCRIPTION & DIALOGUE
	4	Raghab Dutta is seen to come forward in the same way. He is much older. He looks closely at Lalu for a long time and says – **Raghab Dutta**: Here, move away, all of you … let me have a look at him … no, no, it can't be … he is lying – we cremated Lalu before coming back. You are not Lalu … tell us the truth, man … what do you want here?
		CUT
	5	**M.C.S.** Lalu is sitting on the veranda of the courtyard. He speaks in a calm voice – **Lalu**: You people did not cremate me. You floated me in the river when I was half-dead.
		CUT

SC No.	SHOT	DESCRIPTION & DIALOGUE

6 **M.S.**

Raghab Dutta moves towards Nishikanta.

Raghab Dutta: What is he saying!
Nishikanta, you too were present when he was cremated …

Nishikanta: Listen all of you, give this rogue – this fake fakir a thoroughly good beating … he has put on the garb of an ascetic! You scoundrel, you cheat, where were you all this time?

CUT

7 **M.C.S. Composite**

Padmabati is sitting on the veranda of her courtyard.
She looks as if she has gone mad. A few women are holding on to her.

Padmabati: Listen to me, he is really my Lalu, the treasure of my heart … that birth-mark is unmistakable … I have recognised him with absolute certainty …

Phul Thakurani, standing next to her, speaks out –

Phul Thakurani: But how can you take him back in your home, where Radha-Krishna and Lakshmi-Janardan reside? The lad has become an outcaste … it would have been better if he had died …

Thakurani's statement raises a murmur in the crowd.

CUT

8 **M.S.**

Nishikanta: This is an awful mess! I doubt if any expiation or religious service would solve the problem! Losing one's caste is not a minor issue …

CUT

9 **M.S. to M.C.S. (on trolley)**

Lalon rises slowly to his feet. He speaks in a calm voice --

Lalon: How does one lose one's caste—does it escape from the body like air? I would have held on to it had I known.

Lalon picks up his bag as he says this. And then while moving, he says in suppressed anger –

Lalon: If I had my caste in my grip I would have burnt it.

He walks quickly out of the courtyard. People make way for him.

CUT

10 **M.C.S.**
Standing by the door of the room Golapi has been watching the proceedings in the courtyard all this time. Padmabati's lamentations are heard from outside. Golapi lets off a deep sigh.

CUT

29 1 **Location: Bank of a pond**
Time: Afternoon
M.S. (Long focus lens on trolley)
Lalon is advancing towards the pond with his back to the Camera. He is followed by several half-naked urchins of the village. A little irritated, Lalon halts abruptly and turns around. The urchins disperse noisily in various directions.

CUT

2 **M.L.S. to M.S.(Toppish) Camera on Crane**
Still water of the pond. Lalon enters the Centre Frame and sits down by the pond. Back to Camera he drinks water from the pond to quench his thirst. The sound of sipping water from his cupped palms is heard from the Sound track.

CUT

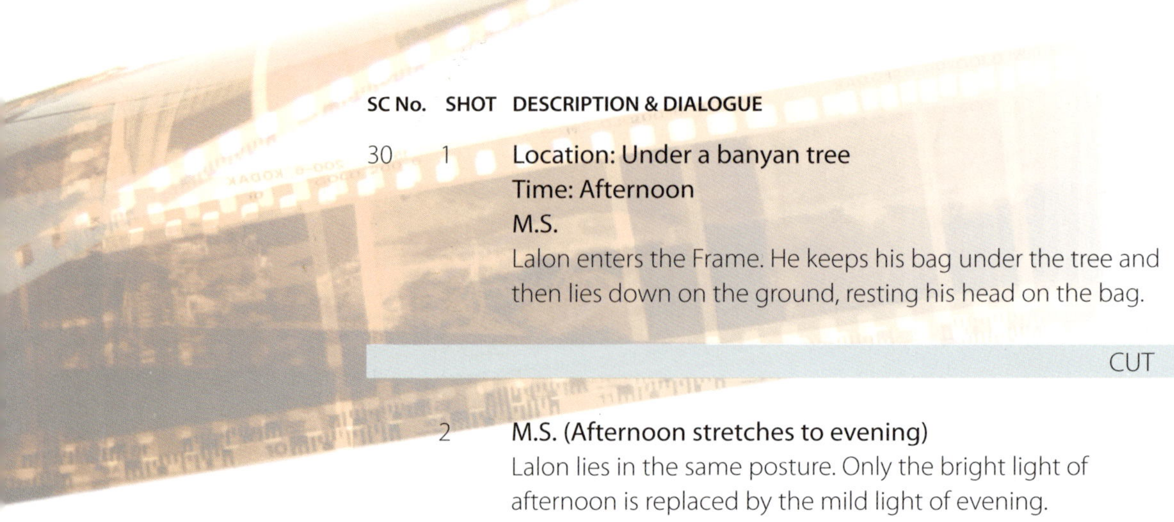

SC No.	SHOT	DESCRIPTION & DIALOGUE
30	1	**Location: Under a banyan tree** **Time: Afternoon** **M.S.** Lalon enters the Frame. He keeps his bag under the tree and then lies down on the ground, resting his head on the bag.
		CUT
	2	**M.S. (Afternoon stretches to evening)** Lalon lies in the same posture. Only the bright light of afternoon is replaced by the mild light of evening.
		CUT

SC No.	SHOT	DESCRIPTION & DIALOGUE
31	1	**Location: Lalu's cottage** **Time: Afternoon.** Padmabati is straining water from boiled rice and sobbing to herself.
		CUT
	2	**M.C.S.** Golapi's hand spreads a banana-leaf on the floor. Padmabati's hand places hot rice, roasted brinjal, salt and pickle prepared with mustard and mango on the banana-leaf.
		CUT
	3	**M.C.S.** **Padmabati**: Go daughter, go and give this food to my son. He must be dying of hunger. But be careful, make sure that you do not touch him.
		CUT

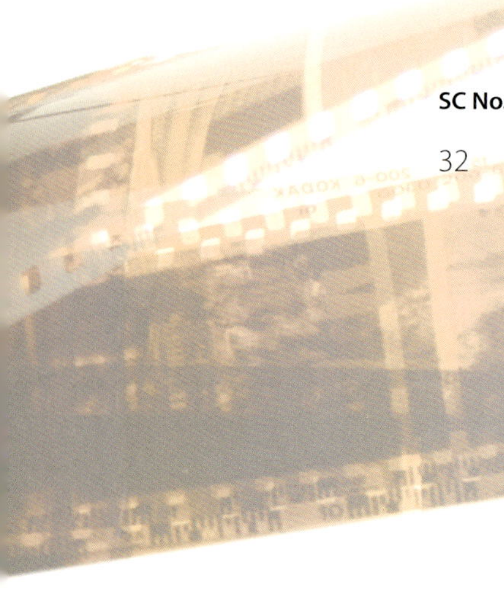

SC No.	SHOT	DESCRIPTION & DIALOGUE
32	1	**Location: Under the banyan tree.** **Time: Dusk.** **M.L.S. (on trolley)** Lalon is sitting under the tree, The light of the descending evening falls on his face. Golapi enters the Frame, the food on the banana leaf in one hand and an earthen pitcher of water in her other hand. She comes to a halt after taking a few steps. Then she advances towards Lalon. **The Camera tracks and composes the two in M.S.** Golapi lays down the food on the ground very carefully and is about to leave. **Lalon**: Please sit down with me for a while dear … please. Golapi sits down a little away from Lalon. Lalon starts eating hungrily.
		CUT
	2	**M.S. to M.C.S.** Padmabati enters the Frame through a gap between the trees. She advances towards the Camera and comes to a halt. As she goes on looking intently at Lalon from some distance her face visibly brightens up.
		CUT

SC No.	SHOT	DESCRIPTION & DIALOGUE
	3	**M.S.** Lalon is eating the food with relish. While eating he starts talking to Golapi— **Lalon**: Please forgive me, dear … Golapi does not reply. **Lalon**: I remembered nothing, dear … When recollections came to me I became a fakir. My Guru Gosain had forbidden me to ever think of returning to the past … but what could I do? I felt a strong urge to see you …
		CUT
	4	**C.S.** Golapi had been sitting with her face lowered all this time. Now she slowly raises her face and looks at Lalon.
		CUT
	5	**M.C.S.** **Lalon**: Would you like to become a companion of my ascetic life? … Would you come with me?
		CUT

6 **M.C.S.**

Padmabati is startled to hear Lalon's suggestion.

Lalon (O.V.): We will go to a place where there is no distinction between Hindus and Muslims …

CUT

7 **M.C.S. (Composite)**

Lalon and Golapi.

Lalon: *Where a single moon lights up the earth—from a single seed all gain their birth.*
Come, let us escape to such a land …

Golapi: But I feel very scared …

Lalon: What is there to be scared of? Leaving behind this suffering of a widow's life, you will come with me to a land where there is only blissful cheer.

Padmabati's voice is heard like a sharp rebuke Off Frame.

Padmabati (O.V.): Lalu!

Lalon and Golapi turn around.

CUT

8 **M.C.S.**

Padmabati enters the Frame from one side and advances towards them.

Padmabati: Go home, daughter.

CUT

9 **M.S. (On Trolley)**

Golapi keeps her face lowered. Lalon gulps down some water from the earthen pot. Then he ignores Padmabati's presence and speaks to Golapi in a calm voice:

Lalon: Oh, my beloved Puny fish, you will come with me, won't you?

An inarticulate reply emerges from Golapi's mouth –

Golapi: I will come …

Padmabati starts fuming and advances closer towards them.

The Camera tracks and catches all three of them in M.S.

Padmabati: Wretched girl, you have been caught up in an infidel's web! You are a Hindu widow and you will become a Muslim's companion! Has he not shared his meals with infidels …

Lalon: Calm yourself, mother. The one who fed me was a woman like you. The one who saved me was a woman like you. Why are you seeking the excuse of religion for no reason?

Then he addresses Golapi –

Lalon: Let's go, wife …

Padmabati: Go home, daughter. Remember, our caste and our religion mean everything to us. You are going to rot in hell if you defy them!

Golapi breaks into a sob. Then as she starts moving away, she says –

Golapi: I won't see you again in this life, dear …

She starts weeping as she runs back towards the village.

The Camera follows her.

CUT

SC No.	SHOT	DESCRIPTION & DIALOGUE
	10	**M.C.S. (Composite) (On crane trolley)** Lalon in Preference. Padmabati in Suggestion. **Lalon**: Go on frittering away your life with caste and religion … He hurls the earthen pot in the pond as he says this. Then he picks up his bag on his shoulder and walks away in the fading light of the evening. **The Camera Crane is lifted up.**
		CUT
33	1	**Location:A pathway by the river-bank.** **Time: Approaching evening.** **M.C.S. (On trolley)** Lalon is walking all by himself along a solitary path. **The Camera track is backing.** A song takes shape in Lalon's mind. The song is heard in Lalon's voice in the background. **Lalon (Song):** *After being treated in this shoddy way* *I know not where to go.* *Would I live in this cracked boat till my last day* *Bailing water as I row?*
		MIX
	2	**M.S. Camera on boat** Lalon is crossing the river. It is a melancholy evening. **Lalon (Song):** *Will the ever compassionate God bestow* *His kindness on this wretched sinner once more* *Or will my days be spent in misery – rowing* *this boat-load of sin aimessly as before?*
		CUT

What is there about that love that I can say?
Lust creeps around it all night and day.
Stripped of lust that love can barely stay,
How can I learn pure love, tell me I pray ...

Bolbo ki shey premer kotha
Kaam hoyechhe premer lota
Kaam chhara prem jotha totha
Noy shey agomon...
Kori kemone shohoj shuddha prem sadhon ...

Scene 35; Shot 3

SC No. SHOT DESCRIPTION & DIALOGUE

34 1 **Siraj Sain's hamlet**

Time: Late evening

M.C.S. to M.S. Composite (On trolley)

The same song is being sung in the background.

Lalon stands with his face lifted upwards, as he sings in time. Other minstrels are accompanying him on the tabla and various instruments. Lalon dances as he sings.

Lalon (Song):

Whom can I blame when I know
That my own lapse has cast me low.
Lalon asks – pray, when may I attain
The blessing of my Sain's feet again.

Lalon bursts into tears as he finishes the song and falls at Siraj Sain's feet.

CUT

1A **Camera tracks and brings Siraj Sain in Frame.**

Siraj Sain picks up Lalon and hugs him to his chest, saying—

Siraj Sain: Foolish boy, why did you have to take a leap into forsaken water?

Siraj draws Lalon closer.

Siraj Sain: Your mind is nearly frenzied in lust — why did you choose to turn this way, dying where you were born one day? My poor Lalon!

CUT

Taking a break: Prosenjit Chattopadhyay in Lalon's costume and make up, walking to the shooting spot, followed by unit members

SC No.	SHOT	DESCRIPTION & DIALOGUE

35 1 **Location: A narrow creek**
Time: Morning
M.S.
Siraj Sain is rowing a small boat. Lalon is sitting on the boat. (The Shot is symbolic, as if the Guru, the boatman is showing the way to his disciple.)

CUT

2 **M.S. Composite**
Siraj Sain: Listen, Lalon, I am pleased with your singing … you have learnt how to compose songs which can raise a storm in the mind's ocean … but you are still not entirely free from the attachment to your family … If you want to become an ascetic you have to discard that, my son.
You have to ripen your unripe body …
you have to free your mind from lust …
you have to play a game of repressing your senses.

CUT

3 **M.L.S.**
Lalon bursts into a few lines of a song, while strumming a single-stringed lute.
Lalon (Song):
What is there about that love that I can say?
Lust creeps around it all night and day.
Stripped of lust that love can barely stay,
How can I learn pure love, tell me I pray …

CUT

4 **C.S.**
Siraj Sain speaks while rowing the boat—
Siraj Sain: That is the real truth. What you now need is a female companion.

CUT

SC No.	SHOT	DESCRIPTION & DIALOGUE
36	1	**Location: Siraj Sain's hamlet** **Time: Night** **M.C.S.** Smoke is rising in the Background. It is hard to say if it is emerging from a cooking fire or from smoking opium. Siraj Sain calls out from off Frame – **Siraj Sain**: *Mayur … From the bottom of the Frame a woman's face enters the Frame. There is a bewitching smile on her lips and her eyes are full of mystery.
		CUT
	2	**M.S. Composite [On Crane]** Siraj Sain and Lalon are both seated in Profile. Mayur advances from behind with slow steps. Siraj Sain tells Lalon – **Siraj Sain**: A peacock's body is blue and its eyes are red. Blue signifies envy and red indicates lust. A woman's heart bears envy and her eyes carry lust … Mayur draws near them and sits down in Centre Frame. Lalon asks Mayur— **Lalon**: Do you women bear envy in your hearts? But you serve others with such sincerity and when you love you love so deeply—I cannot see any envy in you at all … **Mayur**: Can envy be seen with the naked eye? Then she smiles enigmatically and says – **Mayur**: My heart is filled to the brim with envy … Gosain scolds me so often, but still, can envy ever disappear? Casting a sidelong glance at Siraj Sain, Mayur pulls up Lalon with her hand. **Camera Crane is raised.** Mayur starts walking with Lalon in the direction that she had come from.
		CUT

* Mayur: Name signifies a 'peacock' in Bengali as well as in some other Indian languages and dialects

SC No.	SHOT	DESCRIPTION & DIALOGUE
	3	**M.C.S.** Mayur pulls Lalon's hand close to her breasts and continues walking. A few residents of the Out of Focus hamlet are sitting behind them. They are singing with the accompaniment of a two-stringed lute, tabor, tom-tom and cymbals, rehearsing for a performance. Mayur is fondling Lalon's fingers. Siraj Sain's voice is heard Off Frame – **Siraj Sain (O.V.)**: Lalon … Lalon and Mayur come to a halt and then look back. **Siraj Sain (O.V.)**: Come to me … Lalon advances towards Siraj Sain. **Camera does Reverse Trolley.** Siraj Sain advances to enter the Frame and then tells Mayur – **Siraj Sain**: You may go ahead. I will send him to you. Then he speaks to Lalon – **Siraj Sain**: Listen Lalon, you witless boy. The action you are about to indulge in has dreadful consequences! But still an ascetic can extract heavenly bliss from that formidable act … A woman is a consort of happiness … a symbol of the greatest illusion of Nature … She is the mother of creation, existence and destruction and at the same time, she is the all-powerful instrument of both unification and dissolution! To have a dalliance with a woman, who holds all these powers, is by no means an easy task, son. If you consort with her without knowing the significance of her strength, you will be completely destroyed. So, as soon as you realise that she is devouring you, you should start controlling your breath … Remember, holding the drop leads to the summit of love. Now go – Lalon goes out of the Frame. Siraj Sain goes on looking in that direction.

CUT

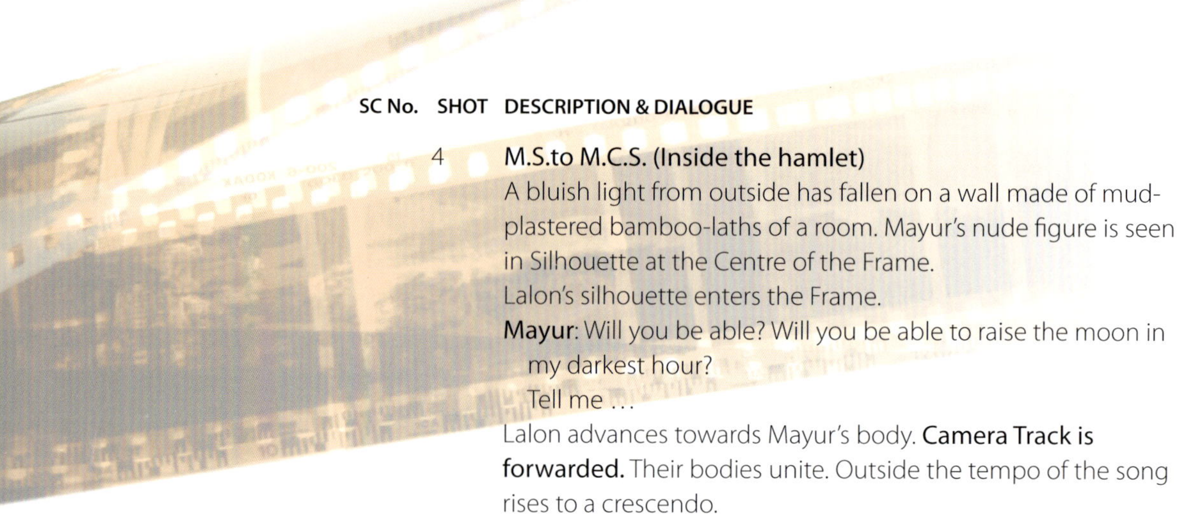

SC No.	SHOT	DESCRIPTION & DIALOGUE
	4	**M.S.to M.C.S. (Inside the hamlet)**

A bluish light from outside has fallen on a wall made of mud-plastered bamboo-laths of a room. Mayur's nude figure is seen in Silhouette at the Centre of the Frame.

Lalon's silhouette enters the Frame.

Mayur: Will you be able? Will you be able to raise the moon in my darkest hour?

Tell me …

Lalon advances towards Mayur's body. **Camera Track is forwarded.** Their bodies unite. Outside the tempo of the song rises to a crescendo.

CUT

SC No.	SHOT	DESCRIPTION & DIALOGUE
37	1	**Location: River-bank adjoining woods.** **Time : Dawn.** **M.L.S. to M.S. On Crane** A small boat advances, piercing the early morning mist on the river. When the boat draws near, it is seen that Lalon is rowing the boat. Lalon's voice as an old man is heard on the Sound Track — **Lalon: (O.V.)**: I floated the boat of my body once again as per my Guru's instructions. I was my own boatman; before me lay an endless ocean. My Guru had told me – 'Go Lalon, go and search yourself, search for human beings, get ten more human beings on your boat … this boat is made of magic wood, there is no fear of its sinking …' CUT
	2	**M.S.** Lalon's boat enters the Frame through a narrow creek. There are thick forests all around. The boat touches the bank. CUT
	3	Lalon is walking along the river-bank. CUT

SC No. SHOT DESCRIPTION & DIALOGUE

4 **M.L.S. to M.C.S.**

Ancient trees tower above others in the forest enveloped in mist. **Camera tilts down to bring Lalon in Frame.** The chirping of birds can be heard all around with the droning of crickets. Lalon is charmed by these sights and sounds. **The Camera follows Lalon's look and pans.** Lalon gets out of the Frame. **The Camera goes on panning the forest.**

Lalon (in old age) (O.V.): My heart was filled with a pleasant feeling at the sight of that beautiful place. I thought to myself that if birds and beasts could live in that place, why shouldn't human beings be able to live there too—particularly people like me who had been driven away by society? I felt an urge to make my home in that forest just the way the birds made their nests …

CUT

5 **M.L.S. to M.C.S. On Trolley.**

Holding on to the branches of a *kapok tree, the Camera tilts down and the trolley is forwarded.

Lalon's face is brought in the Frame as he is seated under the tree. Even though Lalon's face looks delighted in this environment there are distinct signs of fatigue in his eyes. Lalon starts practising the control of breath i.e. *pranayam*, which he had learnt from his Guru. Sitting in the lotus posture he covers his eyes with both hands and closes his ears with his thumbs. Then when he releases his breath the sound of 'Om' emerges from his mouth.

Lalon: Om …

The Camera tracks back to catch Lalon in M.S.

The sound of 'Om' is echoed all over the forest.

MIX

6 **L.S. (Day for Night)**

Gradually the night draws to a close and the sounds of the forest keep on changing. The surrounding areas start looking mysterious in the dim moonlight.

Lalon remains sitting motionless under the tree.

MIX

* Kapok: Also known as the Silk-cotton free (botanical name *Bombax ceiba*; Sanskrit-Shalmoli; Bengali-Shimul) it bears large red flowers. Common in the tropics, of the Baobab family, its wide canopy and tall sturdy trunk are often a shelter for wildlife

SC No.	SHOT	DESCRIPTION & DIALOGUE
	7	**L.S. (Same Camera set-up)** Day-break. Chirping of birds all around. Lalon is seated under the tree.

MIX

SC No.	SHOT	DESCRIPTION & DIALOGUE
	8	**M.C.S.** Lalon is sitting with his eyes closed. His head rests against the tree. He is immersed in a self-absorbed trance. The strain of a song comes floating from a distance. Lalon opens his eyes very slowly. He is still in a trance. He thinks he is having a hallucination. Yet the song draws gradually closer. The words of the song are now clear. **Song (off)**: *Love is so distressing* *That my life now is spent in crying* *All day and night,* *My life is now a living hell—see how* *Love has caused this miserable plight . . .*

CUT

SC No. **SHOT** **DESCRIPTION & DIALOGUE**

9 **M.S.**

Kalua advances, singing.

Song: *He longs and he loves in vain*
And in the end he burns in pain,
Roaming in towns and fairs
like a man possessed ...

The Camera tracks with Kalua. Suddenly Kalua catches sight of someone. His song comes to a halt midway.

Kalua: Here, who are you? And what are you doing here?

CUT

10 Lalon rises to his feet very slowly.

CUT

11 **M.S. (From Lalon's P.O.V.)**

Kalua is seen. He is wearing a loincloth tucked tightly between his legs. His upper body is bare and his face is covered by a thick beard and moustache. He carries a stick in his hand and has a chopper tucked in his waist.

Kalua: I see that you are wearing the garb of an ascetic—were you occupied in meditation?

CUT

12 **M.C.S.**

Lalon: You have a sweet singing voice ... who are you, brother?

Kalua's loud laughter is heard from Off Frame.

CUT

13 **M.L.S. (Toppish) to M.S.**

Lalon and Kalua are seen standing face to face.

Kalua laughs as he says –

Kalua: He asks me who I am. I am a mad man ...

Kalua makes some peculiar gestures as he says this.

SC No. SHOT DESCRIPTION & DIALOGUE

The Camera Crane is lowered.

Lalon breaks into laughter.

Kalua: Why are you laughing? Tell me, why are you laughing?

Lalon: You see, brother, I too am mad!

Kalua is somewhat startled to hear this.

Kalua: Tell me your name.

Lalon: Lalon.

Kalua: Lalon! Are you a Hindu or a Muslim?

Lalon: I am a human being … a mad human being …

Without talking any more Kalua breaks the stick in two on his knees and hands over one piece to Lalon as he says –

Kalua: There can be no quarrel between mad men. Here, eat this …

Lalon had not noticed till now that what he had taken as a stick was actually a piece of sugarcane.

Kalua splits the skin of the sugarcane with his teeth.

CUT

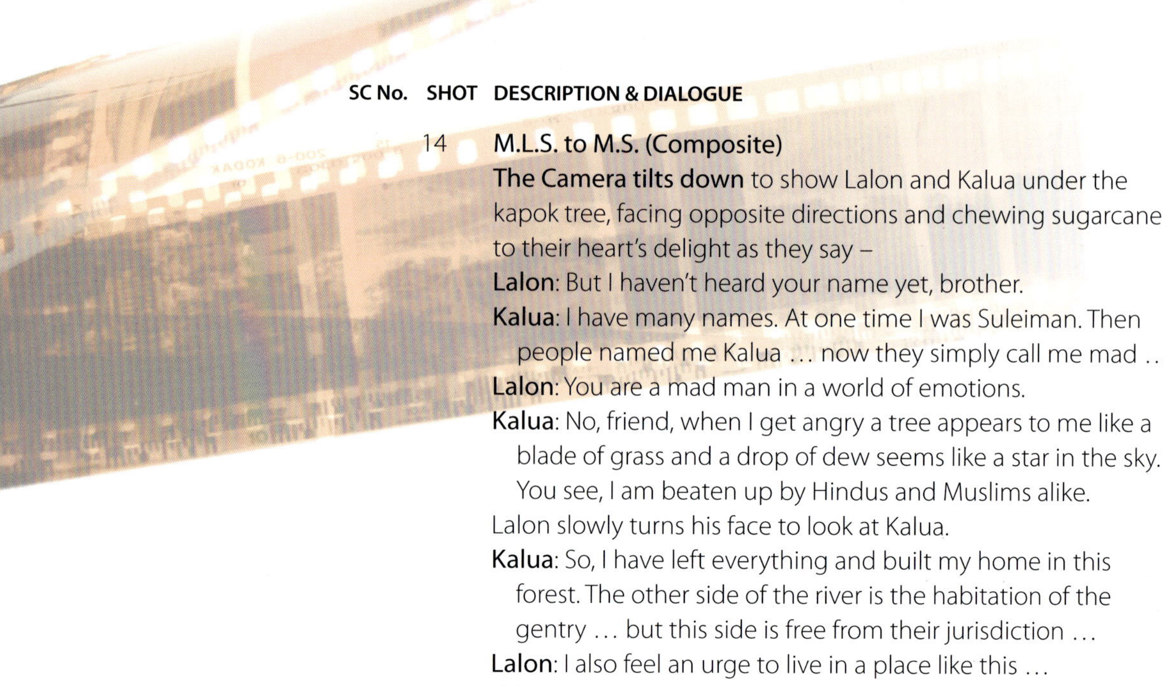

SC No.	SHOT	DESCRIPTION & DIALOGUE
	14	**M.L.S. to M.S. (Composite)**

The Camera tilts down to show Lalon and Kalua under the kapok tree, facing opposite directions and chewing sugarcane to their heart's delight as they say –

Lalon: But I haven't heard your name yet, brother.

Kalua: I have many names. At one time I was Suleiman. Then people named me Kalua … now they simply call me mad …

Lalon: You are a mad man in a world of emotions.

Kalua: No, friend, when I get angry a tree appears to me like a blade of grass and a drop of dew seems like a star in the sky. You see, I am beaten up by Hindus and Muslims alike.

Lalon slowly turns his face to look at Kalua.

Kalua: So, I have left everything and built my home in this forest. The other side of the river is the habitation of the gentry … but this side is free from their jurisdiction …

Lalon: I also feel an urge to live in a place like this …

Kalua abruptly asks –

Kalua: Can you cut bamboos?

Lalon: I can try …

CUT

Take a plunge, oh mind and behold this wonderful view
The one whom you search in heaven and hell
Lies here—in this body before you …

When I get angry a tree appears like a blade of grass to me
And a drop of dew seems like a star in the sky

SC No.	SHOT	DESCRIPTION & DIALOGUE
38	1	**Location: A comparatively clear area adjoining the forest.** **Time: Morning.** **M.L.S. low angle.** Kalua's small hut is seen—built on a tree in the midst of the forest. Kalua enters the Foreground, bearing bamboos on his shoulders. He dumps the bamboos on the ground. The sound of the bamboos striking the ground is heard Off frame, mingling with a tune played on a single-stringed lute. Kalua looks up. Lalon's song comes floating in the air.

CUT

SC No. **SHOT** **DESCRIPTION & DIALOGUE**

2 **Lalon (Song):**

Take a plunge, oh mind and behold this wonderful view
The one whom you search in heaven and hell
Lies here—in this body before you . . .

CUT

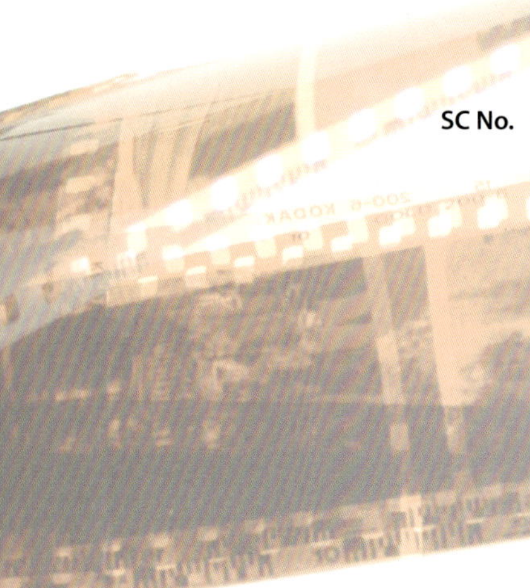

SC No.	SHOT	DESCRIPTION & DIALOGUE
	3	**M.L.S. to M.S.on trolley** Kalua advances towards Lalon. Surprise is written in his eyes and on his face. **The Camera tracks Lalon in the Foreground and brings him in the Frame.** Lalon is playing a one-stringed lute and singing. **Kalua**: But, friend, you never told me that you could compose songs! **Lalon (Song)**: *Just as the first letter of the alphabet* *has a hidden identity* *So does in every human being the Sain* *retain his entity . . .*

CUT

	4	**M.L.S. (Toppish)** Lalon is singing. Kalua starts dancing with arms lifted above his head in rhythm with the song. **Lalon (Song)**: *Why otherwise do all saintly persons* *Bow down their heads to human beings . . .*

CUT

I do not have any caste
only when I become mad ...

SC No.	SHOT	DESCRIPTION & DIALOGUE
	5	**M.S. to M.C.S. Composite. On Trolley** After dancing round and round for some time Kalua comes and sits down beside Lalon. **Lalon (Song):** *A in the alphabet and Mohammad is the first* *Appearing as Siraj Sain on the earth's face.* *Yet Lalon is racked by his bitter thirst* *Ever unquenched without the Sain's grace.*

CUT

	6	**M.L.S.** On hearing Siraj Sain's name Kalua raises his hands to his head and says – **Kalua**: Glory be to the Guru! Lalon finishes the song. **Kalua**: But these lines are from Siraj Sain's song … how did you come to learn them? **Lalon**: This was composed by this humble servant of the Sain, but it was Sainji who spoke through this disciple's mouth … he is my Guru, the lord of my heart … **Kalua**: Please let me touch your feet. You are a disciple of Sainji!

SC No. SHOT DESCRIPTION & DIALOGUE

Lalon: Have you seen Sainji?

Kalua: It was he who drove me mad, but he did not make me his disciple …

Kalua starts crying as he says this, as if overcome by a sudden bout of madness. He rolls on the ground, wailing loudly as he goes on saying –

Kalua: Why didn't you make me your disciple, Sainji?

Kalua's cries are echoed in the woods and forests.

CUT

I haven't seen him for a single day;
In a town of mirrors close to where I stay ...
He is among the many neighbours who dwell
Under a single roof and are yet faring well
I haven't seen him a single day ...

Ami ekdin o na dekhilum taarey
Barir kaachhey arshi nagar
Shetha porshi boshot korey
Ek ghor porshi boshot korey
Ami ekdin o na dekhlum taarey ...

Scene 66; Shot 8

SC No.	SHOT	DESCRIPTION & DIALOGUE
39	1	**Location: River-bank and an adjoining path.**

Time: Early morning

M.L.S. (Toppish) Long Focus lens

The river-bank is seen. Behind it lies a strip of sandy land. In the Foreground of the Frame there is river-water. The stump of a palm tree has been laid to serve as landing stage. A number of bamboos are lying near it. On the other side of the Frame a man is lying with his face on the ground. Next to him sits a young woman clad in widow's clothes. Beside her there is a small bundle and a tin trunk. The young woman notices something and rises to her feet. In the Foreground a small boat loaded with bamboos enters the Frame. Lalon and Kalua are in the boat. The boat reaches the landing stage. Kalua and Lalon are about to unload the bamboos from the boat. The man who had been lying down till then, manages to get to his feet somehow and he advances towards Kalua with tottering steps. His body carries several bruises.

He speaks out in a broken voice –

Man: Suleiman, Suleiman, my dear, please save us …

He falls down on the ground after saying these words.

The young woman stands still, her head covered by her sari.

CUT

SC No.	SHOT	DESCRIPTION & DIALOGUE
	2	The man scrapes along the ground to advance towards Kalua and says – **Man**: Suleiman, Suleiman, my dear, please save us …
		CUT
	3	**M.S. Composite On Crane** In the Foreground Kalua and Lalon are unloading the bamboos from the boat. In the Background the injured man enters the Frame again.
		CUT
	4	**Man**: Suleiman, I am Kashem … please save us …
		CUT
	5	**Kalua**: I am not Suleiman … I don't know you …
		CUT
	6	**M.L.S.** Kalua goes on doing his work. Lalon feels disturbed. Kashem appeals again in a distressed voice – **Kashem**: They have beaten me so hard that my waist is broken. We have somehow made our escape … tell me, who else can we turn to for help except you? **Lalon**: Kalua, the poor man is in such condition … we should do something … Lifting a bundle of bamboos to his shoulders. Kalua says— **Kalua**: You are a fakir … don't pay heed to those squalid people. … Come, let us lift the bamboos, we are already late for the market. Lalon, still perplexed, lifts the bamboos. **The Camera Crane is lifted with them.** In the Background the young widow appears in the Frame.

SC No.	SHOT	DESCRIPTION & DIALOGUE

Kalua tells Lalon –

Kalua: The fellow is in this condition on account of that wench – she is a Brahmin widow … *tchah, tchah*! You are a Muslim and you had to make love to a Brahmin widow … and you thought that they wouldn't beat you, but feed you sweet porridge instead! Go! Go away from here!

CUT

7 **M.L.S. (Toppish)**

A pathway made of clay. Kalua in front and Lalon at the rear, bearing bamboos on their heads, enter the Frame. After they have gone some distance the young widow is seen to enter the Frame. She runs down and stands in front of Kalua, blocking his way.

Kalua and Lalon come to a halt.

CUT

8 **M.C.S.**

In the Foreground stands Kalua with a bundle of bamboos on his head. The young widow is blocking his way.

Komli: They are going to kill us, I beseech you, please do something …

After saying this Komli falls at Kalua's feet. She goes Out of Frame.

Kalua: Get out of my way, Komli, you witch!

Komli rises to her feet slowly and then says in a soft voice—

Komli: You too had made love to me one day, remember? You had fled, but Kashem didn't.

Kalua does not reply.
Lalon speaks in a calm voice from Off Frame –
Lalon (O.V.): Kalua!

CUT

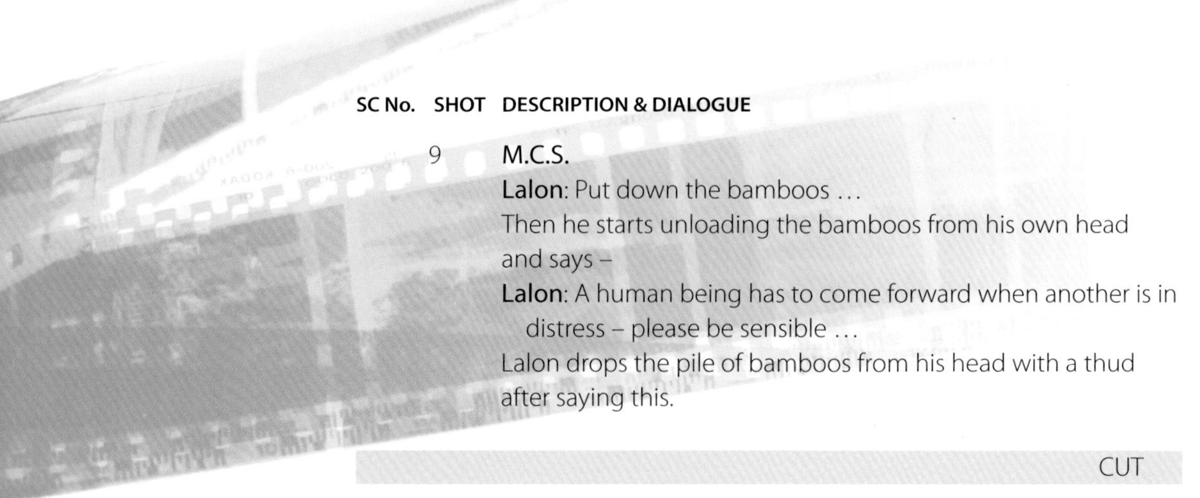

SC No.	SHOT	DESCRIPTION & DIALOGUE
	9	M.C.S. **Lalon**: Put down the bamboos … Then he starts unloading the bamboos from his own head and says – **Lalon**: A human being has to come forward when another is in distress – please be sensible … Lalon drops the pile of bamboos from his head with a thud after saying this.
		CUT

SC No.	SHOT	DESCRIPTION & DIALOGUE
40	1	**Location: Lalon and Kalua's home in a comparatively clear area adjoining the forest** **Time: Afternoon** **M.L.S.** Kashem has been laid down outside a room. A little away from where he is lying rice is being cooked in an earthen pot. After raising Kashem to a sitting posture, Komli advances in the direction of the earthen pot. By the side of his own home Kalua has almost finished building a shed supported on bamboo posts with dried leaves, grass and reed to serve as the roof. Kalua is leaning down on the bamboo posts while working. Lalon stands on the ground, handing over the leaves to him.

CUT

SC No.	SHOT	DESCRIPTION & DIALOGUE
	2	**M.S. Composite** After handing over the last leaf Lalon looks in amazement at the shed built by Kalua and says— **Lalon**: Wonderful, Kalua! You have built a room in thin air in no time! You are brilliant! While still laying the leaves on the roof, Kalua says— **Kalua**: You don't know this, but I was a thatcher before I became mad … I had built so many thatched huts in the village of that Brahmin woman … Lalon looks at Komli.
		CUT
	3	**M.C.S.** Komli hums a song as she works. **Komli (Song)**: *Love is so distressing …*
		CUT
	4	**M.S.** Kalua keeps on looking at Komli
		CUT
	5	**M.C.S.** While humming the song Komli casts a sidelong glance at Kalua. Then she opens the cover of the earthen pot on the oven, stirs the contents with a bamboo twig and says— **Komli**: My cooking is finished, now you may go and wash up …
		CUT
	6	**M.C.S.** **Kalua**: I do not eat food cooked by a Brahmin woman because it would make me lose my caste …
		CUT
	7	**M.C.S.** **Komli**: Oh! He doesn't know how to read the Namaz and he calls himself a Muslim!
		CUT

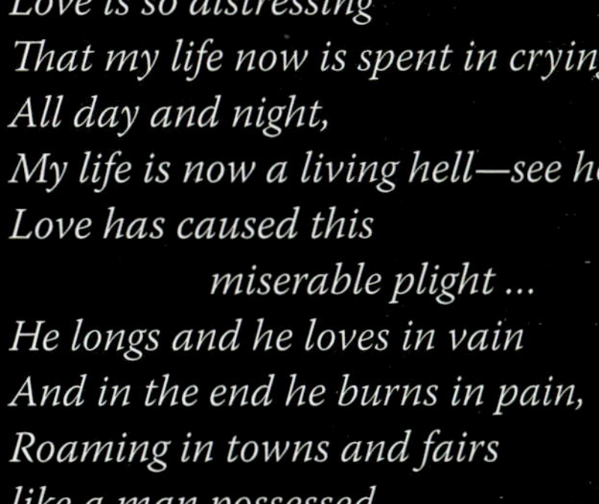

Love is so distressing
That my life now is spent in crying
All day and night,
My life is now a living hell—see how
Love has caused this
miserable plight ...
He longs and he loves in vain
And in the end he burns in pain,
Roaming in towns and fairs
like a man possessed ...

Peeritir eto jwalaton
Kaandte kaandte jonom galo
Jiyante moron
Haye re peeritir eto jwalaton...
Asha korey peerit kore,
Sheshe jwole purey morey
Nogorey bajarey pherey
pagoler moton

Scene 37; Shots 8 and 9

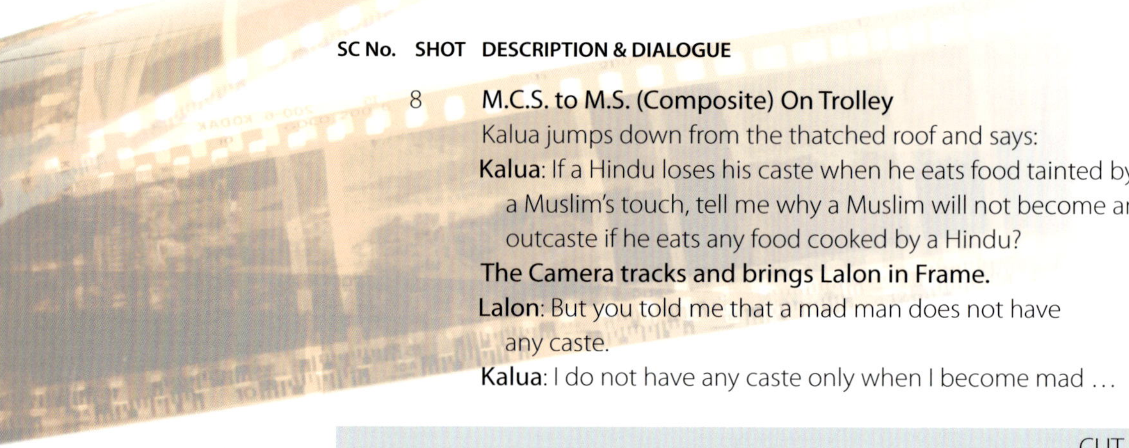

SC No. **SHOT** **DESCRIPTION & DIALOGUE**

8 **M.C.S. to M.S. (Composite) On Trolley**

Kalua jumps down from the thatched roof and says:

Kalua: If a Hindu loses his caste when he eats food tainted by a Muslim's touch, tell me why a Muslim will not become an outcaste if he eats any food cooked by a Hindu?

The Camera tracks and brings Lalon in Frame.

Lalon: But you told me that a mad man does not have any caste.

Kalua: I do not have any caste only when I become mad …

CUT

SC No.	SHOT	DESCRIPTION & DIALOGUE

9 **M.C.S.**

Komli lowers the fire of the oven as she addresses Lalon—

Komli: Would you too lose your caste if you ate any food touched by my hand?

CUT

10 **M.S. Composite**

Komli's question brings about a change in Lalon's expression. He raises his palm in front of his eyes and asks –

Lalon: Does a hand have a caste then?

Then he turns around abruptly and starts walking in the direction of the forest.

CUT

SC No.	SHOT	DESCRIPTION & DIALOGUE
	11	**M.S. Composite** Kalua is surprised at Lalon's reaction. Komli too advances a few steps. **Kalua**: What happened, friend?

CUT

12 **M.L.S.**

On drawing near the forest, Lalon replies.

Lalon: A shoal of puny fish has arrived, my friends, a shoal of puny fish …

Lalon disappears in the forest as he says this.

CUT

13 **M.L.S. to M.C.S. On trolley**

Light and dark environment of the forest.

Chirping of crickets. A song on Lalon's voice comes floating over. **The Camera tracks Lalon and catches him on M.C.S.**

Lalon (Song):

My caste is lost, oh my caste is lost –
its really a strange business!
There is no one who wants to work for truth,
All they know is tum-tess titum-tess …

CUT

14 **M.S. (Long focus)**

Kalua and Komli are seen to advance when they hear Lalon's song. There is Overlapping of Lalon's song.

Lalon (Song):

What was your caste when you came here,
What caste did you take on arrival, dear,
What would be your caste when it's time to go—
Ponder and tell me if you know.

CUT

15 **M.C.S.**

Lalon is singing.

Lalon (Song):

My caste is lost, oh my caste is lost …

The song is now accompanied by music.

CUT

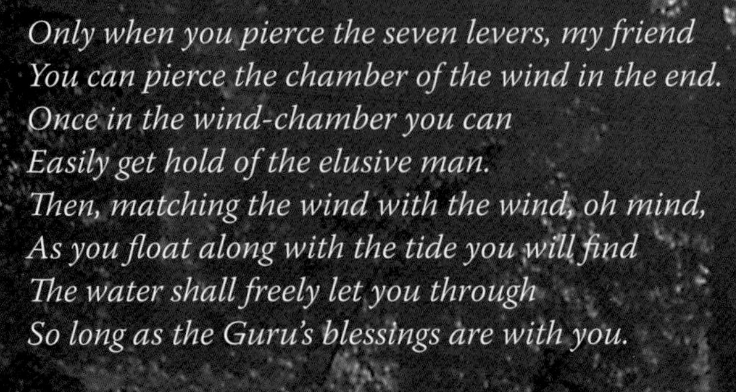

Only when you pierce the seven levers, my friend
You can pierce the chamber of the wind in the end.
Once in the wind-chamber you can
Easily get hold of the elusive man.
Then, matching the wind with the wind, oh mind,
As you float along with the tide you will find
The water shall freely let you through
So long as the Guru's blessings are with you.

Shopto tala bhed koriley
hawar ghorey jawa jaye
Hawar ghorey geley porey
odhor manush dhora jaye
Hawatey hawa mishaye
Jaore mon ujaan beye
Joley bari lagbe narey
Jodi gurur doya hoy

Scene 65; Shot 1

SC No.	SHOT	DESCRIPTION & DIALOGUE
	16	**C.S. (90° Toppish)** Kedgeree in earthen pot. The hands of three men and a woman are taking out kedgeree from the same pot and eating.
		CUT
	17	**M.S. on Round Trolley** Kalua, Lalon, Komli and Kashem are seen taking out kedgeree from the same pot and eating it. (The Song from the previous Shot goes to the Background with the accompaniment of music.) **Lalon (Song):** *A Brahmin, a scavenger, a low-born squatter* *All become purified by a drop of the same water.* *As I see this, I am filled with disgust and mutter—* *Death won't spare anyone, nevertheless ...* *My caste is lost, oh my caste is lost ...*
		CUT

SC No.	SHOT	DESCRIPTION & DIALOGUE
41	1	**Location: Bungalow at Silaidaha** **Time: Night** Lalon of advanced age is playing on a one-stringed lute and singing. **Lalon (Song):** *If someone shares a meal with a whore* *How can it harm his faith or cause a furore?* *What is caste, says Lalon, very few know,* *It's an error unsolved and shall remain forever so.*
		CUT
	2	**M.C.S.** Jyotirindranath is looking at Lalon in utter bewilderment. Sound of Lalon fakir's coughing is heard Off frame. **Jyotirindranath**: Are you people liberalists?
		CUT

SC No.	SHOT	DESCRIPTION & DIALOGUE

3 **M.C.S.**

Lalon smiles a little and says—

Lalon: We are a rudder-less raft on a shore-less river. You can call us a hidden current too – those who want to get lost with us, are free to get lost.

CUT

4 **M.C.S.**

Jyotirindranath: I could not understand properly … who are you talking of?

CUT

5 **M.C.S.**

Lalon smiles briefly and says –

Lalon: These are all poor and distressed people, Babu Moshai, some are even homeless. I do not know how the word had spread that once they entered this forest they could live as they wished.

Your armed footmen don't come to bother them, there is no mullah or priest to threaten them here and there is no discrimination between men and women … You could say, that this is a fairground of joy in the midst of the jungle … a fairground of joy and bliss for expelled people …

DISSOLVE

6 **L.S.**

Lalon's hamlet in the forest

Lalon: A fair of joy for expelled people …

CUT

SC No.	SHOT	DESCRIPTION & DIALOGUE
	7	**M.C.S.** Back to Silaidaha bungalow **Lalon**: But then, it was not always joy and peace … there were fights too …and the fights are still there … fights between the rod and the one-stringed lute … the *ektara*

CUT

Shall I be granted a human life again, my dear?
Make haste, oh mind, while you still exist here.
Sain creates so many diverse shapes in his mould
But none surpasses a human being I am told.
Can you not see even the gods praying for rebirth
To descend as human beings upon this earth
You are fortunate oh mind, that you have been given to float
This human life in the shape of a pretty boat.
Row it with steady hands on this ambrosial ocean
Let your boat not get lost or sunk in a stormy commotion
Shall I be granted a human life again?

Emon manab jonom aar ki hobey
Mon ja kor tworaye kor ei bhobey
Ananto roop srishti korlen sain
Shuni manober uttom kichhu nai
Dakho debota gon korey aradhon
Jonmo nitey manobey
Koto bhagyer pholey na jani
Mon re peyechho ei manab tarani ...
Beye jao twaraye tomar shudharaye
Jeno bhara na dobey ...
Emon manab jonom aar ki hobey

Scene 54; Shot 1

1 **Location: A meadow and a path adjoining a river.**
Time: Afternoon.
M.L.S. to M.S. On Trolley
An old man looking like a fakir is trying to save himself by running across the field. He is being chased by two villagers. Their menacing cries are heard –
Villagers (roar): Here, grab that man … grab him …

CUT

2 **The Camera goes on tracking**. In the Foreground Kalua, bearing articles for a fair on a long, bent pole flung across his shoulders, enters the Frame. He comes to a halt on seeing what is happening.
The Camera tracks to reach Kalua's M.S. position.
Kalua realises at a single glance that a fakir is under attack.

CUT

3 **M.S. Long focus lens 32 FPS**

From Kalua's P.O.V. the old fakir is seen to fall down while running. His pursuers pull off his head-cloth, grab him by his hair and start kicking him. The fakir's screams are heard.

First pursuer: Son of a shaven-headed fakir, where will you escape?

Second pursuer: Let us tear up his lungs … he incites people by singing songs … now we shall stamp down on his throat and stop his singing forever …

CUT

4 **M.S. On trolley**

Kalua lowers the pole from his shoulders, takes out the chopper from his waist and starts running towards the two men. **The Camera tracks the two men beating the fakir and brings them in Frame.** Kalua is about to strike them. Seeing Kalua armed with a chopper, the two men run away. Kalua picks up the old fakir from the ground.

CUT

SC No.	SHOT	DESCRIPTION & DIALOGUE
43	1	**Location: Shimultala** **Time: Morning** **L.S. on Crane** Lalon's retreat in the forest has now taken the shape of a small hamlet. About ten to twelve thatched huts have come up. A platform has been set up in the middle with a thatched roof for holding singing performances. The hamlet is enveloped by a light fog and smoke. The men and women residents of the hamlet are occupied in various chores. CUT
	2	**M.S. Composite** Maniruddin, a man of advanced age, is seen sitting in a room in the hamlet. He is adjusting the strings of his two-stringed lute. **Lalon**: How do you feel now, Maniruddin *bhai*? **Maniruddin**: I am well. It was through Allah's endless kindness that Kalua bhai happened to be there … otherwise they would have killed me … and I have been able to save this lute with great difficulty. **Lalon**: Now, stay with us and enjoy your life … CUT

Setting the stage: On location, the Director supervising the sets of Lalon's Shimultala hamlet in the forests of Chilapata, North Bengal

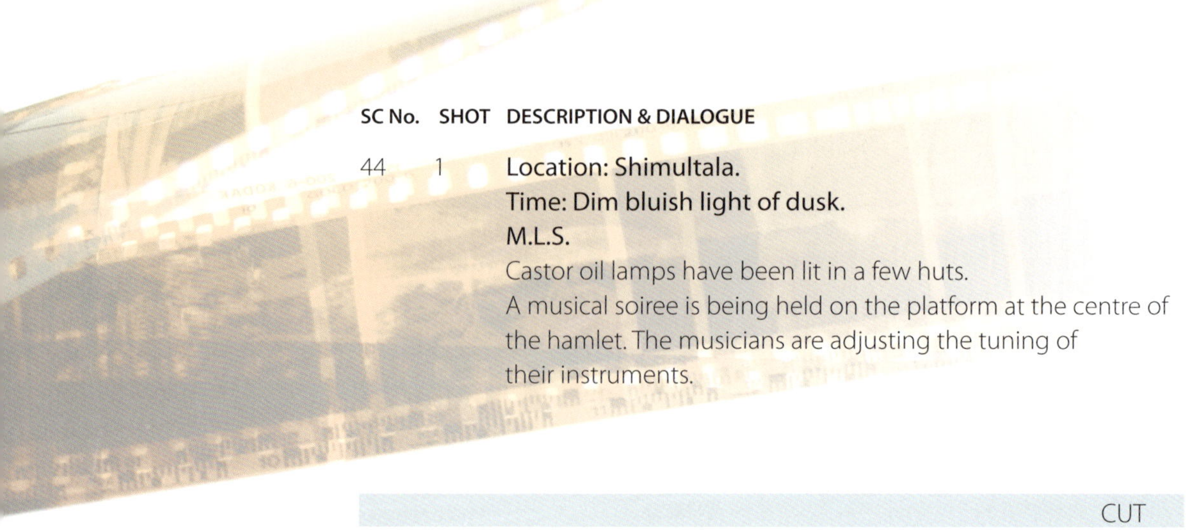

SC No.	SHOT	DESCRIPTION & DIALOGUE
44	1	**Location: Shimultala.** **Time: Dim bluish light of dusk.** **M.L.S.** Castor oil lamps have been lit in a few huts. A musical soiree is being held on the platform at the centre of the hamlet. The musicians are adjusting the tuning of their instruments.

CUT

SC No. SHOT DESCRIPTION & DIALOGUE

2 **M.S. Composite On trolley**

Komli is singing. Kashem is seen among the musicians, bending down slightly to keep in tune with his cymbals. Kalua is beating a tom-tom. Maniruddin is playing on his two-stringed lute. Komli is singing and dancing with a single-stringed lute in her hand. She is wearing a string of bells on her ankles.

Komli (Song):

When I hear that the Sain has set up his abode somewhere
My heart is startled—
like at the sight of a snake appearing from nowhere
—When I hear that the Sain has set up his abode somewhere . . .

A peacock's body is blue and its eyes are red
Blue signifies envy and red indicates lust

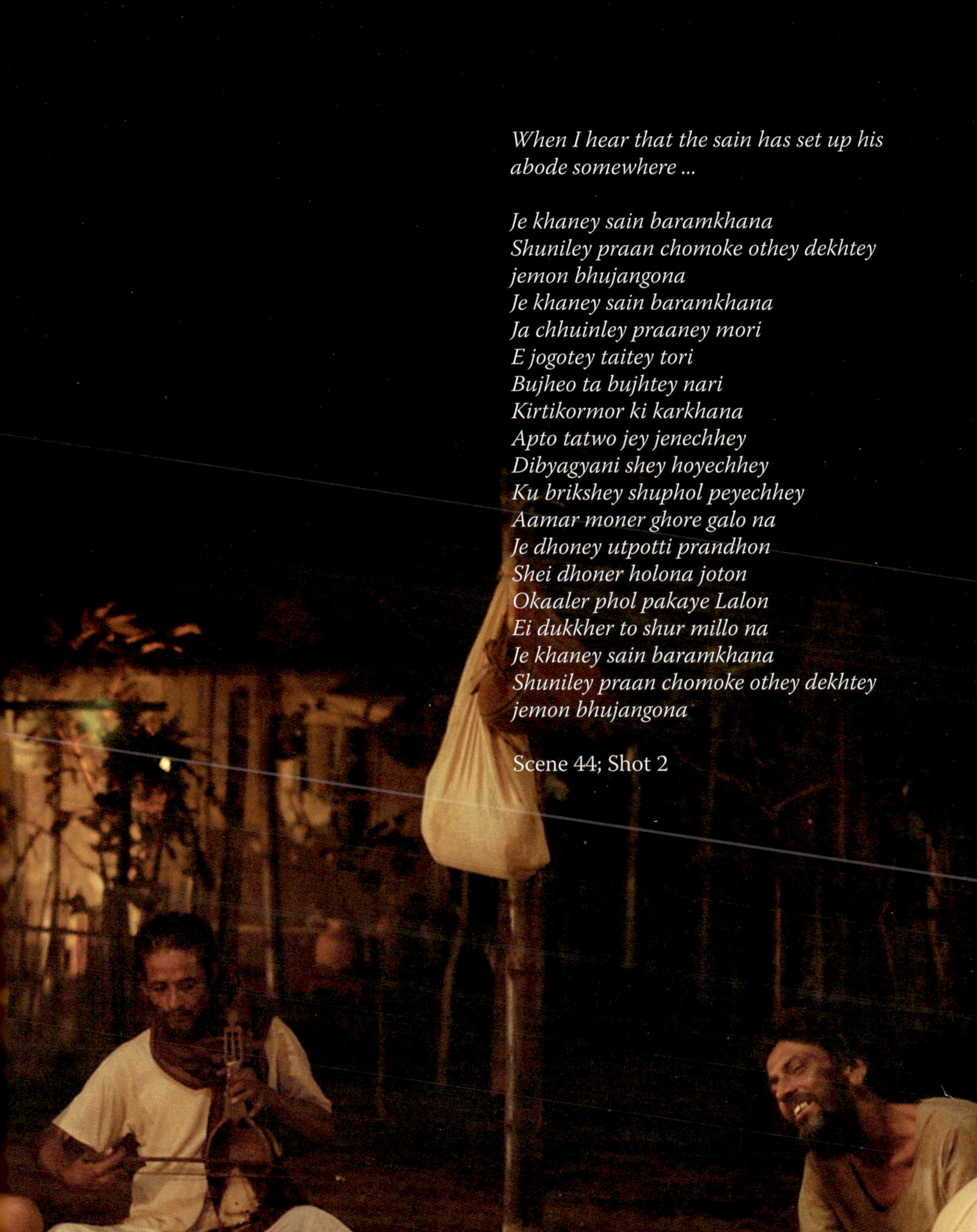

When I hear that the sain has set up his abode somewhere ...

Je khaney sain baramkhana
Shuniley praan chomoke othey dekhtey jemon bhujangona
Je khaney sain baramkhana
Ja chhuinley praaney mori
E jogotey taitey tori
Bujheo ta bujhtey nari
Kirtikormor ki karkhana
Apto tatwo jey jenechhey
Dibyagyani shey hoyechhey
Ku brikshey shuphol peyechhey
Aamar moner ghore galo na
Je dhoney utpotti prandhon
Shei dhoner holona joton
Okaaler phol pakaye Lalon
Ei dukkher to shur millo na
Je khaney sain baramkhana
Shuniley praan chomoke othey dekhtey jemon bhujangona

Scene 44; Shot 2

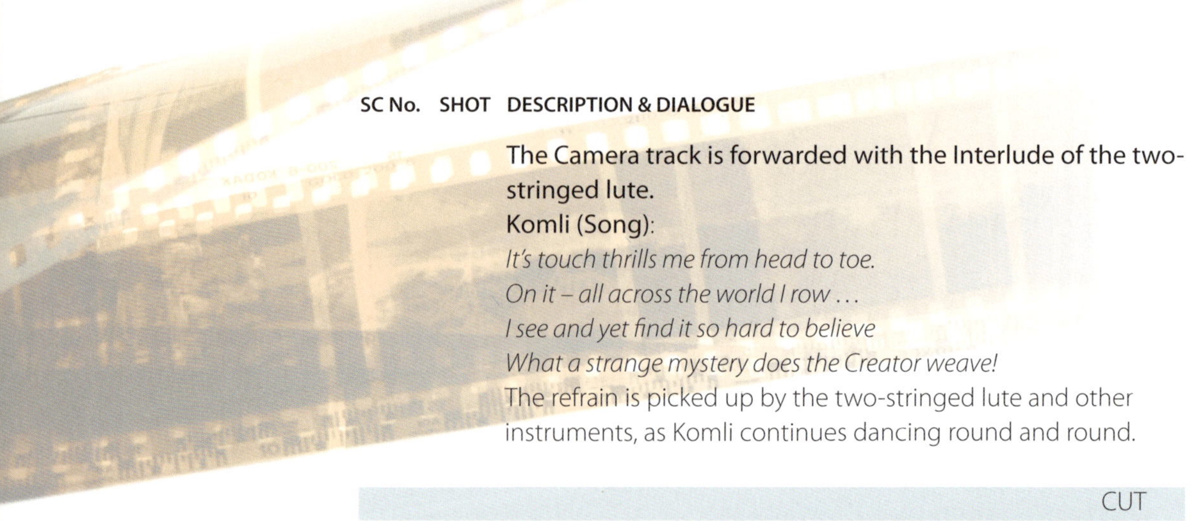

SC No. SHOT DESCRIPTION & DIALOGUE

The Camera track is forwarded with the Interlude of the two-stringed lute.

Komli (Song):

It's touch thrills me from head to toe.
On it – all across the world I row . . .
I see and yet find it so hard to believe
What a strange mystery does the Creator weave!

The refrain is picked up by the two-stringed lute and other instruments, as Komli continues dancing round and round.

CUT

SC No.	SHOT	DESCRIPTION & DIALOGUE
	3	**M.S.: Lalon's cottage in Shimultala** In the dim light of a small oil-lamp Lalon is seen sitting in a lotus posture inside his room. In tune with the refrain of the music outside Lalon sings to himself — **Lalon (Song):** *He who the truth about himself has known* *Has attained supreme wisdom on his own.* *Yet beguiled by the gains of an evil tree* *From dark obsession my mind I cannot free.*

CUT

SC No.	SHOT	DESCRIPTION & DIALOGUE
	4	**M.S.** Komli singing at the soiree. **Komli (Song):** *The source of precious life, alas, isn't given* *The least attention and is not cared for even.*

CUT

SC No.	SHOT	DESCRIPTION & DIALOGUE

5 **M.C.S.**

Lalon sings inside his cottage –

Lalon (Song):

Lalon ripens a green fruit before it's time
But this miserable song can find no rhyme.

CUT

6 **M.L.S.**

Musical soiree. Komli is singing with the accompaniment of music.

Komli (Song):

When I hear that the Sain has set up his abode somewhere
My heart is startled—
like at the sight of a snake appearing from nowhere.

FADE OUT

SC No.	SHOT	DESCRIPTION & DIALOGUE
45	1	**Location: Lalon's cottage in Simultala** **Time: Night** **C.S. to M.C.S. On Trolley Fade In** The light of a small oil-lamp from Close. A part of Lalon's face enters the Frame and blows off the oil-lamp. **The Camera Track goes back.** There is bright moonlight outside, which has trickled into the cottage through the window of bamboo lathes, plastered with clay. Lalon is fully stretched out. The moonlight falls on his face. Lalon goes on gazing outside. He hears a woman's voice humming a song, which seems to draw closer.

CUT

SC No. SHOT DESCRIPTION & DIALOGUE

2 **M.C.S. On Trolley Day for Night**
In the moonlight Komli is seen coming towards Lalon's cottage.

CUT

3 **M.S. On Trolley**
The shadow of Komli's figure falls near the door from
Lalon's P.O.V.
Komli: Sain, haven't you gone to sleep?

CUT

SC No.	SHOT	DESCRIPTION & DIALOGUE
	4	**Lalon (O.V.)**: No, I was watching how the moonlight touches the moon.
		Komli: I wanted to talk to you ...
		Lalon (O.V.): Come in ...
		Humming her song in the background of light and shade, Komli enters the cottage and sits down beside Lalon.
		The Camera tracks and Composes them.
		Komli says in an indulgent tone –
		Komli: Why didn't you come to hear my song?
		Lalon: I did hear it – from a distance ... I had forgotten that song ... it is a song of love and affection, the journey from lust to dispassionate love ...
		Komli: How can love be dispassionate, Sain? Didn't you tell us that a river of lust gets inflamed into a storm with the practice of love!
		As she says this Komli draws closer to Lalon.
		Lalon feels a little uncomfortable as he asks –
		Lalon: Where is Kashem?
		Komli: He sleeps – as if he has become senseless – while I burn all over. Sain, please quench my burning ...
		Then Komli impatiently wraps her arms around Lalon and starts hugging him as if she has gone mad.

SC No. SHOT DESCRIPTION & DIALOGUE

The Camera tracks and moves to M.C.S. with Komli in preference. Lalon keeps sitting like a stone.

Komli: What's wrong? Are you made of stone?
Don't you have any lust or desire?

Lalon: Why shouldn't I? I am just like any other human being.

As he speaks, Lalon's voice gets choked.

From rubbing her face on Lalon's chest Komli lowers her head downwards. The sound of their breathing becomes louder. Suddenly Komli's laugh is heard Off Frame. Then Komli enters the Frame again.

Komli: Now your lust has been aroused! Your desire is strong … you must be making surreptitious raids in amorous domains. Now satisfy me, Sain.

Lalon: The body responds to its own rules, but if the mind does not respond …

Komli's passion crumples. She covers her face with both hands and runs out of the cottage. **The Camera tracks back to retain Lalon in Frame.** Komli leaves behind a trace of silent tears in the cottage. Lalon remains sitting in a dazed state.

CUT

SC No.	SHOT	DESCRIPTION & DIALOGUE
46	1	**Location: Forest and Shimultala adjoining the forest.** **Time: Dawn** **M.L.S. On Crane** The Crane is lowered to show Kalua and Shetal walking across the forest enveloped in mist, bearing bundles of green bamboos. The sound of the blowing of conch-shells floats in from a distance.
		CUT
	2	**M.C.S.** Lalon's Profile. His face is lit up by the first light of dawn. Lalon is blowing a conch-shell. Blowing a conch-shell is yet another exercise for controlling the breath.
		CUT
	3	**M.L.S. (Toppish) Morning On Crane** The women of the habitat are by the river. Some are bathing, some are washing utensils, while Komli is filling water in a pitcher.
		CUT
	4	**M.C.S.** After filling the pitcher, Komli lifts it to her waist and starts walking towards the habitat. Her figure is visible through her wet sari. A song rises spontaneously to Kalua's lips. Komli glances in his direction.
		CUT

200-0 KODAK

5 **M.S. to M.C.S. On Trolley**

Kalua is driving bamboo posts into the ground for erecting a hut. A youth is standing on the ground and handing over material and tools to him. The youth's name is Bholai. The two are humming a song while they are working.

Kalua + Bholai (Song):

La Ilahi Illallah

A law is framed by Rasulullah

The Camera tracks Kalua at work and goes Close to him.

Suddenly Kalua catches sight of Komli. His singing stops.

CUT

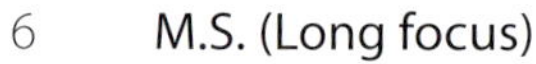

6 **M.S. (Long focus)**

From Kalua's P.O.V. Komli is seen walking in her wet clothes with a pitcher of bell metal on her waist.

Komli stops abruptly and then turns to look at Kalua.

She smiles briefly and says –

Komli: Why did you stop, Mian? Sing on …

CUT

7 **M.S. On Trolley**

In the middle of his work Kalua suddenly becomes violent in anger. In a moment there is a total change in his facial expression. He strikes hard at the bamboo post with his axe splitting it into pieces.

CUT

8 **M.L.S. (Toppish) On Crane**

In his frenzy Kalua is seen bringing down the huts one by one with his axe. People crowd around him and try to pacify him. From time to time Kalua chases them threateningly, saying –

Kalua: Get away from here, get away from here, all of you. I had built these huts and I am going to pull them down myself …

As he says this Kalua stumbles down to the ground, but jumps up to his feet very quickly.

CUT

SC No. **SHOT** **DESCRIPTION & DIALOGUE**

9 **M.S. to M.C.S. (Long focus lens)**

Lalon is seen advancing. He stops on reaching Close to the Camera.

Lalon: Go on … destroy them to your heart's content … destroy them with relish … see if that quenches the fire burning within you …

CUT

10 **M.S. (Low angle) (On trolley)**

Kalua, raving mad, starts crying as he advances towards Lalon. **The Camera tracks back.** Those who had been crowding around Kalua till now, start walking behind him. Lalon enters the Frame.

Kalua: I have gone mad, friend. I am destroying these huts and I shall rebuild them myself …

Kalua throws himself at Lalon's feet as he says this.

Lalon lifts him up with his hands.

Lalon: Do whatever you want to …

Then addressing those who were following Kalua

Lalon says –

Lalon: Please move away, all of you … leave us alone …

Lalon looks in the direction of Komli's hut.

CUT

SC No.	SHOT	DESCRIPTION & DIALOGUE
	11	**From Lalon's P.O.V. the Camera walks towards Komli's hut. The Camera stops in front of the door.** Lalon calls Komli. **Lalon (O.V.)**: Komli …

CUT

	12	Lalon enters the Frame. Komli is combing her wet hair as she comes out from the hut and enters the Frame; she stands in front of the Camera, looking at Lalon. Komli says – **Komli**: Tell me, Sain … Then, lowering her eyes, she says – **Komli**: How may I serve you?

CUT

	13	**M.C.S. Over Shoulder** Lalon in Preference, Komli in Suggestion. **Lalon**: Kalua needs to be with a woman. I want that you should serve him .

CUT

SC No.	SHOT	DESCRIPTION & DIALOGUE
	14	**M.C.S. Over Shoulder** Lalon is in Suggestion, Komli in Preference. Komli smiles briefly and says — **Komli**: But he had left me and fled – such a long time ago … **Lalon**: Time has called him back again …
		CUT
	15	**M.S. to M.C.S. On Trolley** Komli breaks into two lines of a song. **Komli**: *No pursuit can bear fruit* *Once the time is lost …* Then she fixes her eyes on Lalon's eyes and says – **Komli**: I cannot disobey your order … My Sain is well-versed in the art of love … She retreats into her hut after saying this. Lalon gets down from the veranda and proceeds towards his own hut.
		CUT
	16	**M.S. to M.C.S. On Trolley** Kashem is standing by the fence. **From Lalon's Profile the Camera tracks towards Kashem.** Lalon crosses the Camera and goes away. Kashem's eyes are blank. Kalua is sitting with his back resting on a bamboo post.
		CUT

SC No.	SHOT	DESCRIPTION & DIALOGUE
47	1	**Location: River-bank adjoining the forest.** **Time: Misty morning.** **B.C.U.** The float of a fishing line is seen motionless on the water-surface.

CUT

	2	**M.C.S. (Composite)** Lalon's Profile. His eyes are fixed on the float. Behind him is Bholaishah. He too is looking on curiously. **Bholai**: It looks like the whole day will be wasted, they won't take a bite today … **Lalon**: I have cast the fish-hook in Sain's water … whether they bite it or not Bholai, I'll be content if they nibble it just once … Bholai starts humming a song composed by Lalon. **Bholai (Song)**: *Along the bank where three rivers unite* *Like a fish does my Sain abide in delight.* *On the water-surface all day you wander* *Why don't you ever think of going deep under?* **Lalon**: Wonderful! You seem to be a natural poet! **Bholai**: What are you saying, Sain? This song was composed by you!

Lalon: Really? I had forgotten it altogether.

Bholai starts singing again.

Bholai (Song):

While there was time why didn't you raise a pier
Now the river will dry up and the fish diasappear . . .

Lalon's eyes suddenly stray towards the river.

Lalon: Can you see who are coming?

Bholai: Kalua-bhai must have got hold of some new residents . . .

Lalon: No, these people look like gentlemen . . .

CUT

SC No.	SHOT	DESCRIPTION & DIALOGUE
	3	**M.L.S. (Toppish)**

Kalua brings the small boat to the river bank.

A middle-aged gentleman gets off the boat along with a young gentleman. Both are fair-complexioned and dressed in fine clothes. With them there is a lady, whose loose hair is matted. She wears a red dot on her forehead and a string of *rudraksha* around her neck She is accompanied by a youth who is lean and emaciated but has the typical sharp features of a man living in rural areas.

Kalua: Frends, these gentlemen are looking for Lalon fakir's hamlet.

He starts smiling to himself after saying this.

CUT

SC No.	SHOT	DESCRIPTION & DIALOGUE
	4	**M.S. Composite On trolley** Lalon is sitting with the fishing rod in his hand. **Harinath**: Brother, can you tell me where I may find Lalon fakir? Lalon hands over the fishing rod to Bholai and then says with folded hands –
		CUT
	5	**C.S.** **Lalon**: If you please, sir, I am Lalon ... He rises to his feet as he says this. Harinath is a little startled.
		CUT

SC No.	SHOT	DESCRIPTION & DIALOGUE

6 **M.S.**

After surveying Lalon from head to toe, Harinath says –

Harinath: My name is Harinath Majumdar … I am coming from Kumarkhali.

Then pointing to the person standing next to him, he says –

Harinath: And this is my young friend Mir Mosharraf Hossain.

Mir Mosharraf: But the people of this area know him as *Kangal Harinath …

Lalon goes on looking blankly.

Harinath: So many highly placed gentlemen, zamindars and people living in Calcutta and Dhaka know me … and you haven't even heard my name!

CUT

7 **C.S.**

Lalon replies in the same humble manner –

Lalon: No sir.

CUT

8 **M.S.**

Now Harinath bursts into loud laughter and says –

Harinath: I am not a man of distinction by any means … I am the humblest of the humble, I am neither wealthy nor do I have the honour of being highly educated … and yet some people know my name … do you know why? Because I bring out a newspaper under the title *Grambarta Prabashika* (Rural News Reporter) in which we write about the misery and distress of the farmers and the common rural folk … have you ever read our newspaper?

CUT

9 **M.S.**

Lalon: Sir, it is my misfortune that I have not been able to have much book-learning … so, I beg you to forgive me …

CUT

* Kangal: Poor, a beggar

* Zamindars: Landlords

Behind the shots: Prosenjit Chattopadhyay (Lalon) helps out with the make-up of Chanchal Chowdhury as Kalua at an outdoor location

10 **M.S.**

Harinath: Tell me, why are you addressing me as sir ? Am I your master or your patron? And you obviously do not know your own worth. Are you aware that your songs are now on the lips of people in every village?

CUT

11 **M.S. Composite**

Bargakshepi and Duddushah are standing on the boat.

Harinath: And these people have also come to hear your songs … Bargakshepi …

Bargakshepi touches her hands to her forehead in *pranam* and says –

Bargakshepi: Glory be to my Guru!

Harinath: And Duddushah

Duddushah acknowledges the introduction by offering a *salaam*.

CUT

12 **M.C.S. Composite**

Harinath and Mir Mosharraf. The forest is seen in the Background.

Harinath: Fakir sahib, where is your hamlet?

CUT

13 **M.C.S.**

Lalon: If you please, it is not too far … it is inside that forest … a very short boat-ride along a canal … why don't you come and see it?

CUT

14 **M.C.S. Composite**

Mir Mosharraf: A singer's hamlet inside a forest! That's a strange concept! I am very curious.

Lalon (O.V.): Kalua, please escort these gentlemen. I'll be with you shortly.

CUT

15 As Kalua rows a small boat, carrying the guests to the opposite bank, he starts singing.

Kalua (Song):

Now Kali it is you I am going to devour –
With the string of skulls on your neck
I'll cook a delicious broth,
Tasting sweet and sour . . .
Kali, it is you I am going to devour . . .

SC No. **SHOT** **DESCRIPTION & DIALOGUE**

48 1 **Location: Lalon's hamlet inside the forest**
Time: Afternoon. On Trolley

Arrangements have been made for serving lunch to the guests on the raised dais. Komli and Shetal are serving the food. Rice and lentil soup have already been served. While eating Mir Mosharraf says—

Mir Mosharraf: I wanted to ask you – since you people have set up your hamlet inside this forest, has the Zamindar granted you any lease-hold rights?

Lalon: I do not know …

Mir Mosharraf: This entire forest land falls within the zamindari of the Thakur family – don't you know that?

Lalon: I have heard of the Thakur family … but then this forest is a gift from the Almighty God …

Harinath: The Almighty God is no doubt the supreme authority, but if we have to live in this world we have to bow down our heads to the zamindar, the magistrate and the police. And no rights can be acquired without paying the right price …

CUT

SC No. SHOT DESCRIPTION & DIALOGUE

2 **M.C.S.**

Lalon: But we are powerless to pay any price.

CUT

3 **M.S. Composite**

Mir Mosharraf: Look, what I would suggest is that you may call upon the Thakur family and arrive at some understanding. They are highly educated and respectable, but they are also very strict about levying taxes ...

Harinath: The present Zamindar, Debendranath Thakur is worshipped as a great saint by one and all both here and abroad. Till he attained sainthood his poor subjects still had some means of approaching him for redress of their grievances and he used to shower his kindness on them too. But now that he has become the principal guru of the Brahmo society ...

CUT

4 Lalon listens in amazement.

Harinath: These days he is so busy with the formless Absolute Being ...

CUT

5 **M.S. Composite**

Harinath: He has no time to listen to his poor subjects.

He has left everything to his steward and to his employees …

Mir Mosharraf: They might send their armed footmen any day and throw you out from here …

Harinath: So, you have to come out from your cage and get to know this world.

CUT

6 **M.C.S.**

While eating Lalon smiles softly and says:

Lalon: But babu, this whole world is a spherical cage which goes on revolving all day and night …

CUT

7 **M.S. Composite On Trolley**

Lalon's Profile in Foreground. Harinath and Mir Mosharraf beside him.

Harinath: How did you know that the world is spherical and goes on revolving?

Lalon: I do not know, but wise and learned people say so …

Harinath is overcome with surprise.

Mir Mosharraf changes the topic and asks Lalon—

Mir Mosharraf: Tell me, fakir sahib, is Lalon a Muslim name? And what is your full name?

CUT

'How does the
unknown bird
Enter the cage
and easily exit
If I could hold it,
I would tie
my mind
As a chain
around its feet

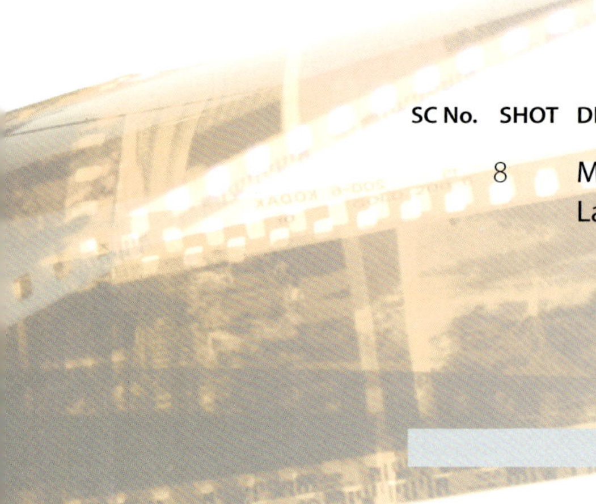

SC No.	SHOT	DESCRIPTION & DIALOGUE
	8	**M.S. On Trolley** **Lalon**: I do not have a full name. I am an ordinary man … this short name is enough for me. I do not have the power to hold the divine designs of Allah or the Almighty God in my small head. Till now I haven't been able to understand human beings properly and I do not even know myself …
		CUT
	9	**M.S.** **Harinath**: Know thyself – this is an age old theory …
		CUT
	10	**Lalon**: I do not understand all these theories, babu. And when I cannot explain my thoughts in words some songs appear from nowhere in my mind. Just now when you mentioned a cage, a few lines of a song came flocking to my mind …
		CUT
	11	**M.S. to C.S.** Lalon breaks into a song – **Lalon (Song)**: *How does the unknown bird enter the cage and easily exit?* *If I could hold it I would tie my mind as a chain around its feet.*
		CUT

SC No. SHOT DESCRIPTION & DIALOGUE

12 **M.C.S. Composite**

Harinath is overwhelmed with emotion and says –

Harinath: This is a wonderful song, fakir sahib!– The unknown bird in a cage!

Then he addresses Mir Mosharraf and says –

Harinath: Such deep thoughts … I did not know that they could be expressed with such ease … he is a mystic poet, isn't it so, Mir?

Mir nods his head without displaying much emotion.

CUT

13 **M.S. Composite**

Harinath speaks again in an overwhelmed voice –

Harinath: But my thirst is growing stronger. I have an urge to stay here tonight and hear your songs.

Mir Mosharraf: Harinath-*da*, we can't stay much longer here … the editorial has to be completed early tomorrow …

Harinath: That is true. We will take leave of you today, fakir sahib, but we will come some other day …

Bargakshepi: We would like to stay for a few days … with the Sain. We can learn some songs and music, what do you say, Duddu?

Lalon says in a humble voice –

Lalon: That would be good, I too will be able to learn from you …

CUT

Blessed is he
who has built a house, raising walls in emptiness
On a single post the house is set
With no soil at its base and yet
It resists storms with rare finesse.
Blessed is he …
In the house there are nine rooms spread in a cluster
And above them an attic finished in rough plaster
There a mad fellow sits all alone with his Master.
Blessed is he …
On top and bottom, side by side
There are nine and a half doors and still
Lalon says – I can go inside
Through any of them at will.
Blessed is he …
Dhonyo dhonyo boli taarey
Bendhechho emono ghor shunyer upor posta korey

Ghorer shobey matro ekti khunti
Khuntir goraye naire maati
Kishey ghor robey khanti jhor tufaan eley porey
Dhonyo dhonyo boli taarey ...
Muladhar kuthri noyta
Taar uporey chileykotha
Tahe ek pagol beta boshey eka ekeshwarey
Dhonyo dhonyo boli taarey
Upor neechey shari shari
Sharey noy dorja taari
Lalon koy jetey paari
Kon dorja khuley ghorey
Dhonyo dhonyo boli taarey

Scene 61; Shot 1

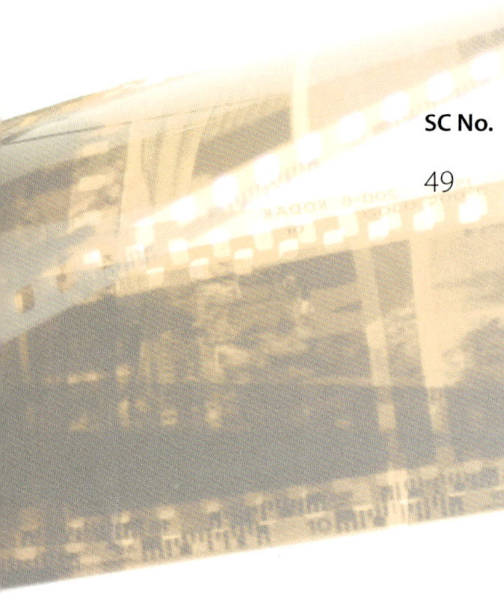

SC No.	SHOT	DESCRIPTION & DIALOGUE
49	1	**Location: River bank** **Time: Late evening.** **M.L.S. to M.S, On Trolley** **The Camera is tracking above the trees and bushes in the forest. The Camera tilts down and goes on tracking.** Harinath and Mir Mosharraf are going back. Lalon, Maniruddin, Bholai and Shetal have come to see them off. They are walking with their backs to the Camera

Lalon: Do come again …

Harinath: We thoroughly enjoyed the whole day today. You must call on this poor man's home some day. We shall have songs and music there as well. And do please keep a close watch on Baragakshepi, her actions are not always predictable …

Shetal: That is evident from her name.

Lalon: Please do not worry. We have many such mad people in our midst.

CUT

SC No. **SHOT** **DESCRIPTION & DIALOGUE**

2 **M.L.S. Composite On Trolley**

The Camera is Side tracking with them. Trees and bushes of the forest are visible through the Foreground.

Harinath: Fakir sahib, there is something else which I would like to tell you. You people are living happily and peacefully in this new environment with your song and music … which is good. But as you know, this world dotes on the strong and oppresses the weak. When the word is spread that the people of this hamlet know only how to dance and sing but do not know the art of self defence – just like those shaven-headed mystics … you will see that you will be attacked in a clandestine manner from several directions.

CUT

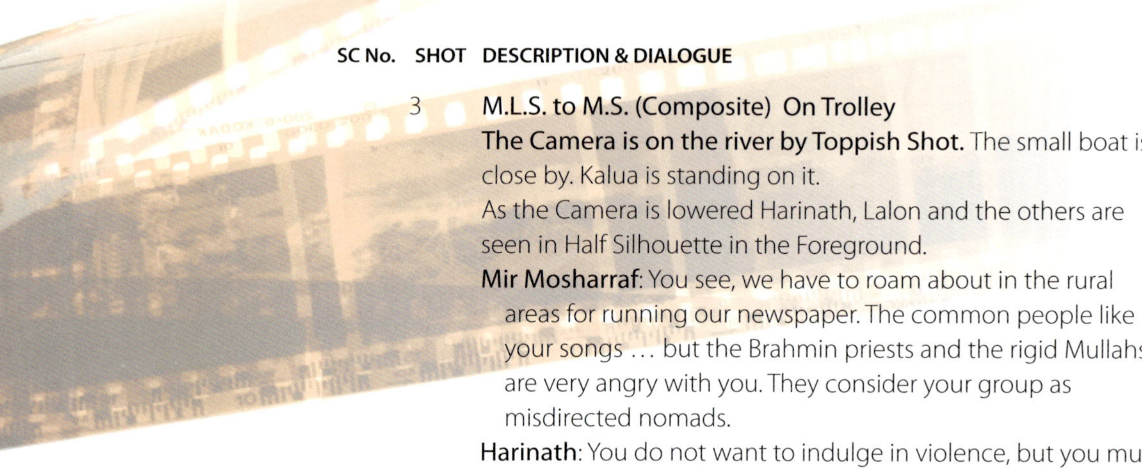

SC No.	SHOT	DESCRIPTION & DIALOGUE
	3	**M.L.S. to M.S. (Composite) On Trolley**

The Camera is on the river by Toppish Shot. The small boat is close by. Kalua is standing on it.

As the Camera is lowered Harinath, Lalon and the others are seen in Half Silhouette in the Foreground.

Mir Mosharraf: You see, we have to roam about in the rural areas for running our newspaper. The common people like your songs ... but the Brahmin priests and the rigid Mullahs are very angry with you. They consider your group as misdirected nomads.

Harinath: You do not want to indulge in violence, but you must acquire the power to resist violence .

CUT

SC No.	SHOT	DESCRIPTION & DIALOGUE
50	1	**MONTAGE** **Location: An open ground adjoining the hamlet.** **Time: Morning.** **M.S.: On Trolley.** **Extreme 90° Low Angle.** The clashing of sticks in progress within the Frame. **The Camera tracks to show Shetal** in the middle of two parallel rows. He is watching the clashing of sticks.
		CUT
	2	**M.S. (Top shot) 90° angle.** Practice of fighting with sticks is in progress.
		CUT

SC No.	SHOT	DESCRIPTION & DIALOGUE
	3	**M.S.(Same as Shot 1)** Fighting with sticks is in progress.
		CUT
	4	**M.S. (Top Shot) 90° angle (Same as Shot 2)** Practice of fighting with sticks is in progress.
		CUT
	5	**M.L.S. (Toppish) On Crane** Lalon and the other male members of the hamlet are all learning how to fight with sticks. **The Camera is lowered.** **Lalon (V.O.)**: We took up sticks on the advice of our friend, Harinath. We also learnt to ride on bamboo stilts and roamed the forests, trudging through woods and thickets with ease. Wild beasts would be scared of us …
		CUT
	6	Lalon is learning to ride on bamboo stilts.
		MIX TO
	7	**M.L.S. Low angle Day for Night** In the light and shade of a moonlit night a few tall shadows resembling trees are seen to advance.
		CUT

SC No.	SHOT	DESCRIPTION & DIALOGUE

51 1

Location: Shimultala
Time: Morning
M.S. Composite

Seated on the dais Lalon is preparing for the daily practice session of song and music. Bargakshepi and Duddushah are also seen among them.

Duddu: Sain, I have a question. Many mullahs and elderly men are displeased because we sing these songs, They abuse us in filthy language and even want to beat us up. They say that it is a sin for a Muslim to sing songs.

Lalon: If the mullahs or the elders declare that singing is a forbidden action, do not enter into any argument with them. Arguments will lead you nowhere. Hold your ears and tell them, 'Sir, I have committed a mistake, please forgive me. I will never sing in your presence again'. Then you can sing to yourself and distribute the nectar of music to those who are thirsty.

CUT

2

M.C.S.

Duddu: But I did not get a proper reply to my question. Is singing permissible or forbidden?

CUT

SC No. SHOT DESCRIPTION & DIALOGUE

3 **M.C.S.**

Lalon: You may bear in mind – not for the sake of arguments but for your own information – that it is not forbidden in the *hadith*. – Listen, I will tell you a story. I had heard this from my Guru Siraj Sain …

CUT

4 **M.S, Composite**

Everybody listens eagerly to Lalon's narrative.

Lalon: During the Id festival a slave-girl was playing drums and singing in the presence of Bibi Ayesha Siddika, while Hazrat was resting. Just then Abubakar arrived and taken by surprise, started scolding the slave-girls, saying—'What is this! Satan's song in Rasul's chambers!' At that point Hazrat turned around and said – 'There is no harm in singing and playing drums on Id day as long as there are no evil temptations.'

Bargakshepi: Glory be to my Guru!

Lalon: Maniruddin bhai, let me see how you explain this to these friends.

Maniruddin starts singing a meaningful song.

Maniruddin (Song):

Why was the sky trembling in sudden emotion?
Why was the earth dancing with reckless passion?
Why was the great Pir perspiring all over that night
As Khaja's song raised the Pir and Aoliya to a glorious height?
Isn't lack of knowledge another name of ignorance?
Yes, and you call it evil if you do not know the difference.

CUT

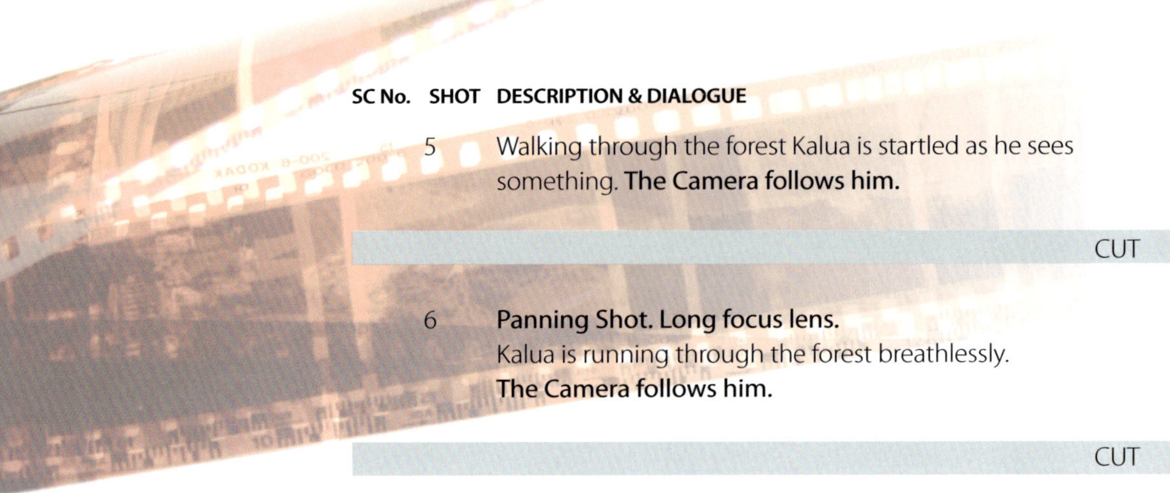

SC No.	SHOT	DESCRIPTION & DIALOGUE
	5	Walking through the forest Kalua is startled as he sees something. **The Camera follows him.**
		CUT
	6	**Panning Shot. Long focus lens.** Kalua is running through the forest breathlessly. **The Camera follows him.**
		CUT
	7	**M.C.S. (Low Angle)** Maniruddin is singing.
		CUT

SC No.	SHOT	DESCRIPTION & DIALOGUE

8 **M.S. Composite**

Seated on the dais Lalon is listening to Maniruddin's song along with the others. when Kalua rushes madly into the Frame and collapses on the ground. Then he says breathlessly—

Kalua: What a shocking thing! Some people are about to burn a woman alive – a young widow – by the river bank. I saw it with my own eyes just now ...

All those who are seated on the dais are startled and they rise hastily to their feet.

CUT

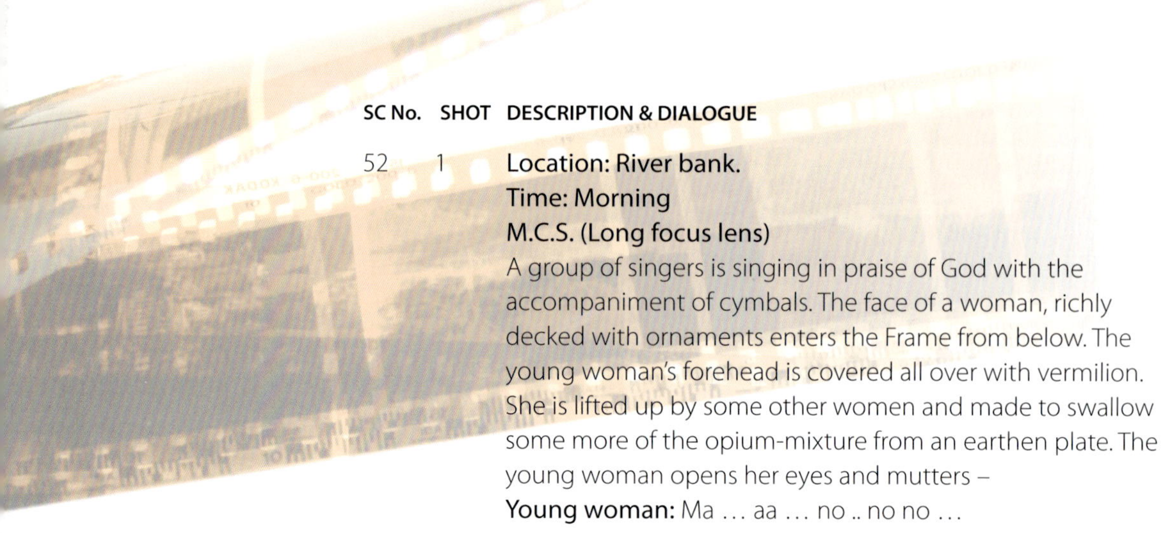

SC No.	SHOT	DESCRIPTION & DIALOGUE
52	1	**Location: River bank.** **Time: Morning** **M.C.S. (Long focus lens)** A group of singers is singing in praise of God with the accompaniment of cymbals. The face of a woman, richly decked with ornaments enters the Frame from below. The young woman's forehead is covered all over with vermilion. She is lifted up by some other women and made to swallow some more of the opium-mixture from an earthen plate. The young woman opens her eyes and mutters – **Young woman:** Ma … aa … no .. no no …

CUT

2 **M.L.S. (Toppish)**

Setting up of the funeral pyre by the riverside is almost complete. The body of the dead man has been laid on the pyre. A priest is chanting hymns. The singers are singing songs in praise of God. Women from the dead man's family are escorting the young woman towards the pyre. Suddenly the young woman makes an inarticulate sound and flops down on the ground with a thud. The dead man's son is seen encircling the pyre before lighting the fire and performing *mukhagni.*

* *Mukhagni*: Hindu cremation ritual of bringing the flame in contact with the lips of the deceased before lighting the fire

CUT

SC No.	SHOT	DESCRIPTION & DIALOGUE
	3	**M.S. Low angle** The symbolic singeing of the dead man is completed. The pyre is now on fire.
		CUT
	4	**M.C.S. On Trolley** The young woman is lifted up. Her eyes are heavy with drugs. She starts moving towards the pyre like a winded doll. **The Camera tracks back.**
		CUT
	5	**M.L.S. (Toppish) Same as Shot-2** The pyre bursts into a blaze. The chanting of hymns and the singing reach a crescendo. The young woman is being taken towards the pyre.
		CUT

The real and the unreal: The Director on location with actors Paoli Dam (left) and Shuvra Kundu playing Komli and Bhanumati respectively, in the film

6 **M.L.S.**

Riding on bamboo stilts, Lalon's group is advancing towards the cemetery.

CUT

SC No. SHOT DESCRIPTION & DIALOGUE

7 **M.S. Composite On Trolley**

The pyre is burning in the Foreground. People from the deceased man's family, the family-priest and the Brahmin singers are scared as they see the advancing group of men. One of them says –

First Man: Are they the *Company's sepoys? Let's get away from here …

Second man: They are going to put all of us in jail …

The priest winds his holy thread around his fingers and screams out in a cursing tone –

Priest: Let me see how much power the Company holds! A Brahmin's curse shall destroy them and their whole dynasty!

Then he grinds his teeth in anger and says —

Priest: Fling the woman in the fire …

* The Company: The British, East India Company

CUT

SC No.	SHOT	DESCRIPTION & DIALOGUE
	8	The panic-stricken men somehow manage to drag the priest along with them as they hurriedly make their escape. Even while being dragged away the priest goes on hurling chastisements. The remaining people run away quickly. **The Camera tracks and moves the pyre from the Foreground.** The young woman stands in a daze for a few moments; then she feels dizzy and collapses on the ground.

CUT

SC No.	SHOT	DESCRIPTION & DIALOGUE
	9	**M.S. Reverse angle** Lalon and his men descend from their bamboo stilts and advance. The group comprises Lalon, Shetal, Kalua, Duddu and Bholai. The pyre is burning on one side. On the other side the young woman is lying in a semi-conscious state. Lalon's group approaches the young woman.

CUT

	10	**M.C.S. to M.S. Composite On Trolley** **Camera at Ground level.** The young woman is lying flat on her face. Her long hair is spread in a tangle on the ground. Lalon and his men sit down on the ground. **The Camera tracks back to bring them in the Frame.** **Lalon**: Go and fetch some water … **Kalua**: What a terrible thing! Has not the Company banned the burning of widows at their husbands' pyres by enacting a law? **Shetal**: No law works in this wretched country … people violate the law surreptitiously … **Lalon**: Hurry – get some water. Duddu fetches an earthen pitcher left behind by the earlier group. Pouring out some water from the pitcher he sprinkles it on the face of the young woman.

CUT

SC No.	SHOT	DESCRIPTION & DIALOGUE

11 **M.C.S.**

As water is sprinkled on the young woman's face, she opens her eyes in her dazed state and asks in a garbled voice –

Young woman: Where am I? Have I arrived in heaven?

CUT

12 **M.S. Composite**

Shetal: Sain, from her appearance she seems to be a married woman from a good family. Should we take her to the police station?

Duddu: She is not yet fully conscious … they must have fed her a good deal of opium …

Lalon: It is necessary to restore her … come, let us take her to our hamlet … go and fetch the mat on which they had brought the dead body …

CUT

13 **L.S.**

Lalon's party is proceeding along a dyke. Four of them are carrying a mat fitted to a bamboo-frame on which the young woman has been laid. The rest are walking with the bamboo-stilts in their hands. They are advancing towards their hamlet in Shimultala.

CUT

53 1 **Location: Shimultala**
Time: Evening
M.C.S. (Toppish)
The young woman has been laid on a bed-sheet made of patchwork on the veranda of one of the cottages. She has not yet recovered from the influence of opium. She is sleeping with her mouth wide open like a dead person. A hand-fan goes in and out of the Frame.

CUT

2 **M.S. (Composite)**
Komli is sitting near the head of the young woman and fanning her. A little away from her Kashem is sitting on his haunches. Lalon is sitting close to the young woman's feet.
Kashem: Why don't you change her dirty clothes?
Komli: Let her regain her consciousness a bit and I'll change them …
Komli had hardly finished the sentence when the young woman tries to get up in a hurry (just the way one does after waking up from a dream). Komli holds her. The young woman mutters to herself –
Young woman: Where is this place? Have I been sent to heaven? Or is this hell? Have they sent me to hell then?
Komli: You are all right …
Komli slowly lifts her to a sitting position.
Young woman: Is this hell? Have I been sent to hell?

SC No. SHOT DESCRIPTION & DIALOGUE

Komli: This is neither heaven nor hell. You are not dead ...
Suddenly the woman starts striking her chest in a frenzied manner and asks –
Woman: I did not die! Why didn't I die?
Then seeing the unknown faces around her she screams out—
Woman: Who are you people?

CUT

3 **M.C.S. Composite On Trolley**
Komli's Profile in Foreground. In Semi-profile the young woman is looking at Komli and trembling violently.
Lalon is seen between the two women. He is observing the helpless girl with a steadfast look.
Woman: Where is my husband?
Komli: He has been burnt to ashes ...
The woman starts screaming as if she has gone mad.
Woman: Strike me ... strike me to death ...
Komli draws her closer and says –
Komli: Foolish girl! Why would you die? Nobody would strike you here ...
Woman: I have nobody ... I have nothing ... let me burn in the pyre ...
Komli consoles her and says –
Komli: You are fortunate to have been born as a human being ... why should you die, dear?
You will see so many beautiful things as long as you live ... so many divine acts ... come, let me take you inside ...
Komli wraps her arms around the young woman and takes her into her room. **The Camera Tracks Forward to reach Lalon's M.C.S.** He is lost in deep thought.

CUT

'Have I been sent to heaven? Or is this hell? Have they sent me to hell then?

I do not know when the bird flies away
Struck by an ill wind the cage begins to sway
Inside the cage the rod breaks and collapses,
Where would the bird perch now–
I try to guess
As I sit and think my mind is seized
with wonder
And feverish amazement grips my body,
tearing it asunder

Pakhi kokhon jani urey jaye
Ekta bod hawa legey khanchaye
Khanchar ara polo dhoshey
Pakhi aar darabey kishey
Ami oi bhabna
bhabchhi boshey
Amar chomok jora
boichhey gaye

Scene 58; Shot 7

54 1 **Location: The river bank in Shimultala**
Time: Late evening
M.S. (Toppish)
Lalon enters the Frame and walks down to sit by the river-bank **Back to Camera**. Then he starts singing to himself –

Lalon (Song):
Shall I be granted a human life again, my dear?
Make haste, oh mind, while you still exist here.

CUT

SC No.	SHOT	DESCRIPTION & DIALOGUE
	2	**M.C.S. Composite Reverse Angle**

Lalon in Foreground. Duddu and Bholai advance silently from the rear and sit down behind Lalon.

Lalon (Song):

Shall I be granted a human life again, my dear?
Make haste, oh mind, while you still exist here.
Sain creates so many diverse shapes in his mould
But none is better than a human being, I am told.
Can you not see even the gods praying for rebirth
To descend as human beings upon this earth?

Duddu: What you said is absolutely right, Sain. What is it that attracts the gods to be born as human beings?

Lalon: I did not say anything. Didn't you hear Komli tell that young girl – 'It is a stroke of luck that you have been born a human being.' That is what made my mind speak out –

Lalon breaks into song again –

Lalon (Song):

You are fortunate, oh mind, that you have been given to float
This human life in the shape of a pretty boat.
Row it with steady hands on this ambrosial ocean
Let your boat not get lost or sunk in a stormy commotion.
Shall I be granted a human life again, my dear ...

CUT

SC No.	SHOT	DESCRIPTION & DIALOGUE

55 1 **Location: An improvised bridge made of bamboos (across a creek)**
Time: Morning.
M.L.S. (Toppish) On Crane

People of two communities, Hindus and Muslims have collected on the two opposite banks of the bridge. On one side is the family priest seen earlier, who is accompanied by several Brahmins with long, slim tufts of hair on the back of their shaven heads. Also seen with them are some well-built men in *dhotis* worn up to their knees. On the other side of the bridge stands the local Maulavi, a few important-looking men and some robust Muslim youths. A joint meeting of Hindus and Muslims is being held to protest against the waywardness of the fakir minstrels. The family priest is quite excited.

Priest: Come, everybody, today we are going to settle this matter once and for all.

Maulavi: Purutmoshai, keep your head cool – these matters have to be dealt with cool heads.

CUT

2 **M.S.**

Priest: Tell me, how can I keep my head cool? Just think, she was a chaste widow through whose piety, not just her family, but everybody in our village would have benefited … oh, how the divine consort was whisked away by that gang of shaven-headed fakirs who came out of the forest to entice that widow away. She was decked in ornaments from head to toe …

Maulavi: You are fretting for the ornaments, Purutmoshai, but their business is to seduce wenches. Even young women from our village have started deserting their husbands and fleeing with those so-called fakirs. The practices followed by these brazen-faced fellows are ill-founded. They do not follow the dictates of Islam, they are bigots. But as you can see, there is a lot of difference even between your grievances and ours …

CUT

SC No.	SHOT	DESCRIPTION & DIALOGUE
	3	**Priest**: My heart rends with shame and disgrace, Maulavi sahib! This woman had the rare opportunity of accompanying her husband to heaven in the same pyre, but no … something has to be done to redress all this …

CUT

4 **M.C.S.**

Maulavi: And the leader of these shaven-headed rascals is that heretic Lalon Fakir. He misguides people. Do you know what he says? He claims that Rasululla and Khudatila are not different – they are two portraits of the same figure! He has even been heard to say that it was Allahpak who appeared in the shape of Rasul to visit this earth. Stupid, ignorant fellow!

CUT

5 **M.S.**

Priest: Yes, their ringleader is that fellow – Lalon Fakir. He has set up a den in the middle of the forest for planning all these evil deeds. I have an idea, Maulavi sahib, but it wouldn't be proper to disclose it in the presence of all these people …

As he says this the Priest moves a few steps close to the Maulavi.

CUT

6 **M.S. Composite**

In his excitement the Maulavi too draws closer to the Priest to say something.

Their Profiles come close to each other from two ends of the Frame.

Priest: Watch out, Maulavi sahib – don't let your shadow fall on my body …

Maulavi comes to a halt while advancing. The Priest talks in a whisper –

Priest: Let us call upon the Steward of the Thakur family to solicit our grievance. We will tell him that this gang of vulgar libertines has forcibly occupied their land and is indulging in many heinous activities to ruin our society …

Maulavi: We too will go to our Imam and ask him to issue a mandate …

As he says this the Maulavi draws closer to the Priest and the shadow of his enormous bulk falls upon the Priest's body.

Priest: Now see what you have done, Maulavi sahib! Your shadow has fallen on me! Tell me, where would I get Ganga water here to purify myself?

CUT

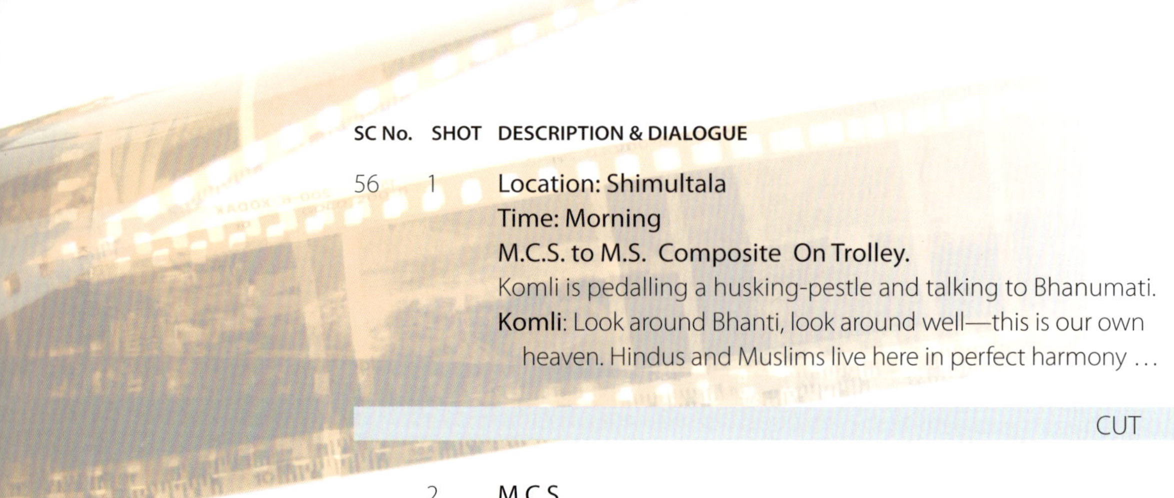

SC No.	SHOT	DESCRIPTION & DIALOGUE
56	1	Location: Shimultala Time: Morning M.C.S. to M.S. Composite On Trolley. Komli is pedalling a husking-pestle and talking to Bhanumati. **Komli**: Look around Bhanti, look around well—this is our own heaven. Hindus and Muslims live here in perfect harmony …
		CUT
	2	M.C.S. Bhanumati is picking up the grinded paddy and keeping it in a wicker-basket.
		CUT
	3	M.C.S. **Komli**: I hope you do not have any fetish about untouchables and such stuff. Because I do not want to deprive you of your faith and make you lose your caste …
		CUT
	4	C.S. **Bhanumati**: What is your religion?
		CUT

SC No.	SHOT	DESCRIPTION & DIALOGUE

5 **Komli**: Earlier I was a Brahmin's wife … now my husband is a Muslim …

Then she smiles a bit to herself and says –

Komli: There are some people here who are neither Hindus nor Muslims … or, they could be said to belong to both religions …

CUT

6 **C.S.**

Bhanumati has a flabbergasted expression on her face as she speaks –

Bhanumati: That sounds incredible! How could it be possible?

CUT

7 **M.C.S.**

Komli and Bhanumati.

Komli: You will see it with your own eyes … some worship idols, some read the namaz … and then there are some who do nothing …

Bhanumati does not respond. The sound of pedalling the husking-pestle is heard.

CUT

8 **M.C.S.**

Komli: What do you wish to do? Would you like to stay here or go back?

CUT

9 **M.C.S.**

Bhanumati: Where will I go?

Then she sighs deeply and says –

Bhanumati: I am not sure …

CUT

SC No.	SHOT	DESCRIPTION & DIALOGUE
57	1	**Location: Shimultala** **Time: Night (Dusk and day for night to be combined)** *** L.S. (To be shot in the Evening)** **M.S. On Trolley** Kalua is seen moving towards a hut in pale moonlight. **The Camera tracks him.** Kalua says in an undertone – **Kalua**: Komli … Komli dear … Komli comes out of the hut and says – **Komli**: You can go and sleep with Kashem on the dais. Bhanumati is sleeping with me. **Kalua**: But I am very hungry, dear … **Komli**: There is puffed rice in a wicker-basket in that other hut. Go and eat some and then go to sleep … Kalua has nothing to say after hearing Komli's reply. He goes on looking meaningfully at her for a while before going out of the Frame. Komli advances a couple of steps. **The Camera tracks back.** Her face is touched by the soft moonlight as she looks up at the sky.

CUT

SC No.	SHOT	DESCRIPTION & DIALOGUE
	2	**M.L.S. Long Focus Lens** The moon has risen in the eastern sky.
		CUT
	3	**M.C.S.** Profile of Lalon sitting at the edge of a pond. His face is lit up by moonlight. Lalon leans towards the water and says – **Lalon**: Have you seen Lalon, what a pretty sight! There is no response.
		CUT

4 **M.L.S.**

Sitting at the edge of the pond, Lalon leans towards the water. The moon is seen in the Background.

Lalon: Why aren't you talking?

CUT

5 **M.L.S.**

The moon's reflection is swaying on the water-surface.

CUT

6 **M.S.**

The voice of Lalon reflected on the water-surface is heard.

Lalon reflected on the water surface: Noor! It is so bright and yet it does not dazzle the sight. This light must be shrouded by an illusion.

CUT

7 **M.C.S.**

Lalon's Profile. Lalon nods his head in concurrence.

Lalon: This Noor drops down on the father's head. Then it is called the seed. That seed enters the mother's womb and is transformed into a red chinarose … and what drops down from the mother's womb upon the earth is Adam. Do you know and understand all this?

CUT

8 Lalon on the water-surface starts singing –

(Song):

*How shall I tell you the *Noor's ways?*
Wrapped all in itself the Noor stays.
Try to hold it and it escapes in a trice
Like a streak of lightning across the skies.

CUT

* Noor: Divine light.

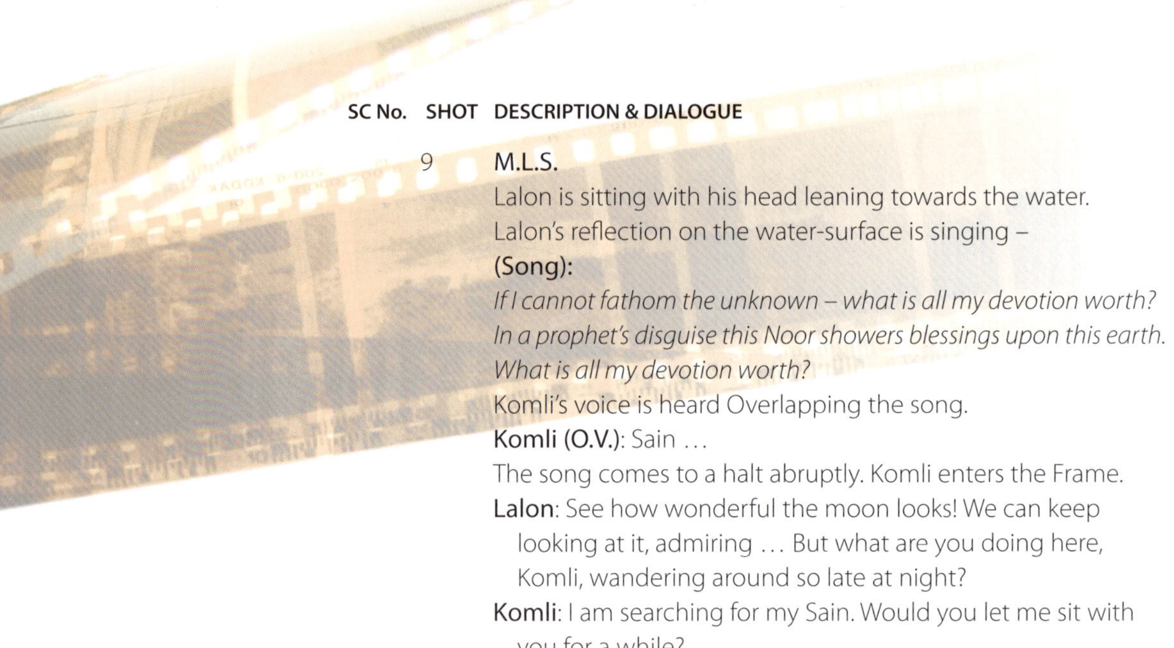

SC No.	SHOT	DESCRIPTION & DIALOGUE
	9	M.L.S. Lalon is sitting with his head leaning towards the water. Lalon's reflection on the water-surface is singing – (Song): *If I cannot fathom the unknown – what is all my devotion worth?* *In a prophet's disguise this Noor showers blessings upon this earth.* *What is all my devotion worth?* Komli's voice is heard Overlapping the song. **Komli (O.V.)**: Sain … The song comes to a halt abruptly. Komli enters the Frame. **Lalon**: See how wonderful the moon looks! We can keep looking at it, admiring … But what are you doing here, Komli, wandering around so late at night? **Komli**: I am searching for my Sain. Would you let me sit with you for a while? **Lalon**: Sit down then. Komli walks down to sit beside Lalon.

CUT

SC No.	SHOT	DESCRIPTION & DIALOGUE

10 **M.S. Composite Reverse Angle**

Komli: Did I interrupt your thoughts?

Lalon: No, so many thoughts crowd in my head all day and night … and they get lost too …

Komli: Would you promise to do something I ask, Sain …

Lalon casts a glance at Komli.

Komli: I want you to accept Bhanumati. After all, you do need someone to attend to your needs … and how many matters can I look after myself?

Lalon smiles a bit and says—

Lalon: But you are the mistress of Shimultala …
All right, send her to me …

CUT

11 **M.S.**

A fish strikes the water of the pond with its tail, making a loud splashing sound.

CUT

58 1 **Location: Shimultala**

Time: Dawn

M.C.S. to M.S. On Trolley

Yellow flowers have come to bloom in front of Lalon's hut. Lalon's hand is carefully loosening the soil with the help of a bamboo twig. A few dead leaves are being sorted out and thrown away. His hair lies loose. Behind him smoke is emerging from the hut.

CUT

2 Lalon goes inside the hut. Bhanumati enters the Foreground with her Back to the Camera. After walking a few steps she turns and looks back. She seems a little hesitant. She carries a small bundle in her hand. Now Komli makes her entrance.

Komli: Go on …

Bhanumati starts moving towards Lalon's hut.

CUT

3 **M.S.**

On entering the hut Lalon squats down on a coarse mat of bamboo slips. Then he starts blowing on a conch-shell.

CUT

4 **M.S.**

Bhanumati comes and stands in front of the door with the bundle in her hand. The blowing of conch-shell continues. Bhanumati remains standing in a confounded manner.

CUT

5 **M.S.**

Lalon finishes blowing on the conch-shell. He notices Bhanumati standing beside the door.

CUT

6 **M.S.**

Bhanumati enters the hut hesitantly. She advances a few steps, halts and says —

Bhanumati: From today I am your serving maid …

Lalon: Come …

CUT

SC No.	SHOT	DESCRIPTION & DIALOGUE
	7	**M.S.** Lalon smiles and says – **Lalon**: Sit down … Bhanumati enters the Frame and remains standing. Lalon says again – **Lalon**: Sit down … Bhanumati hesitates a little and then sits down. As she places the bundle on the floor there is a clinking of ornaments. **Lalon**: Are you happy here – in our village? **Bhanumati**: What are you saying, Sainji? This village is like heaven. No one ever speaks a harsh word to me – this is an experience which I have never had before – either at my parents' place or at my in-laws' house … **Lalon**: Our village is a fairground of joy. But you have to hold on to this spirit of joy … Bhanumati's eyes start glistening with tears. **Bhanumati**: They would have burnt me alive … had you not rescued me … **Lalon**: But it was not I who rescued you … a few human beings got together to rescue another human being. That is why we sing songs in praise of human beings.

CUT

SC No. **SHOT** **DESCRIPTION & DIALOGUE**

8 **M.C.S. On Trolley.**

Bhanumati: I have learnt a song from Komli-*di* …
May I sing it for you?

Lalon: Please do.

Bhanumati (Song):

I do not know when the bird flies away–
Struck by an ill wind the cage begins to sway

The Camera tracks to reach Lalon's M.C.S. Lalon picks up up his one-stringed lute. His face brightens and then he closes his eyes.

CUT

SC No.	SHOT	DESCRIPTION & DIALOGUE
	9	Bhanumati (Song): *Inside the cage the rod breaks and collapses.* *Where would the bird perch now – I try to guess.* *As I sit and think, my mind is seized with wonder* *And feverish amazement grips my body, tearing it asunder.* **While the song is in progress the Camera tracks and reaches Bhanumati's M.C.S.** Bhanumati (Song): *I do not know when the bird flies away* *I ponder but can reach no conclusion in the end . . .* After singing thus far Bhanumati forgets the next line. Realising this Lalon picks up the song immediately— Lalon (Song): *I ponder but can reach no conclusion in the end* *Who owns the cage and who is the bird I cannot comprehend . . .*

CUT

SC No. SHOT DESCRIPTION & DIALOGUE

10 **M.S.**

While singing Lalon signals Bhanumati to join him.

Lalon/Bhanumati (Song):

I ponder but can reach no conclusion in the end
Who owns the cage and who is the bird I cannot comprehend

Lalon and Bhanumati sing together—

Lalon/Bhanumati (Song):

Living with me within my compound
They hold me– to amaze and confound ...

Lalon stops here. Bhanumati continues singing.

I do not know when the bird flies away
Struck by an ill wind the cage begins to sway ...

CUT

11 **Lalon**: Excellent! Where did you learn to sing?

Bhanumati: I belong to Chuadanga, where people start singing devotional songs from the day they are born ...

Bhanumati: Sainji, will you accept me?

Lalon: Stay as you are now. I'll think about it later ...

CUT

‘Our job is to search for the gold held deep inside our minds

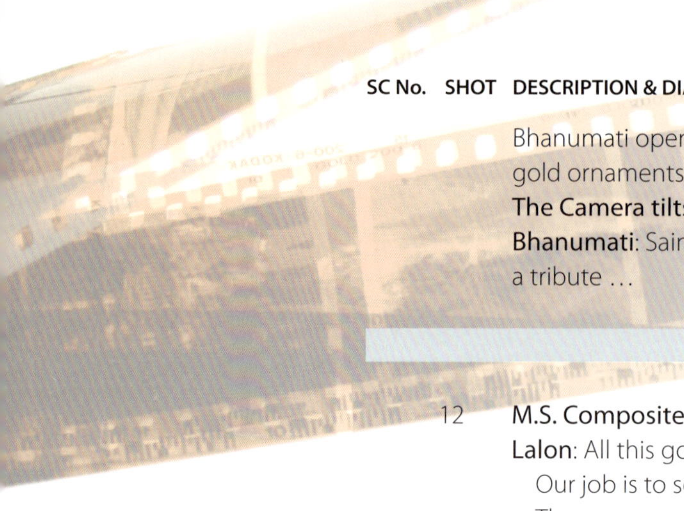

SC No. **SHOT** **DESCRIPTION & DIALOGUE**

Bhanumati opens the bundle and takes out the gold ornaments.

The Camera tilts up to reach Bhanumati's M.C.S.

Bhanumati: Sainji, I wish to deliver these ornaments to you as a tribute …

CUT

12 **M.S. Composite**

Lalon: All this gold and jewellery are not for me, Bhanumati. Our job is to search for the gold held deep inside our minds. These ornaments are meant for your adornment. Keep them with you … wear them when you feel like …

Bhanumati drops the ornaments she had taken out into the bundle. There is a clinking sound once again.

Lalon: And you should devote yourself to your singing. I will introduce you to a devotee.
You will be his partner in devotional practice.

CUT

SC No.	SHOT	DESCRIPTION & DIALOGUE
59	1	**Location: Hamlet in Shimultala** **Time: Morning** **M.C.S. to M.S. On Trolley** Duddu, dressed in white clothes, is sitting in a room of the hamlet. Bhanumati sits before him, her head resting on Duddu's chest, her eyes closed. Duddu has both his arms around Bhanumati, his chin rests on Bhanumati's head. A ray of sunlight has entered through a slit in the roof to fall on their faces. **The Camera tracks forward to reach their M.C.S.** Duddu is looking straight ahead.

CUT

60 1 **Riverside (Bania river)**

Time: Late evening.

M.S.

Lalon is sitting alone on the bank of the river, his eyes fixed towards the sky. The sound of something approaching by the river makes him turn around.

Lalon: You people seem to have hauled up the whole market and brought it here …

Shetal, Kalua, Bholai and two other men are unloading the purchases from the boat. Their semi-silhouettes are seen in the background of the river. Komli and Shetal are advancing. Komli has a basket on her head and Shetal is carrying a loaded sack on his back.

Shetal: It is the day of our grand festival. There will be so many guests. Don't we have to serve them some proper food?

CUT

SC No.	SHOT	DESCRIPTION & DIALOGUE
	2	**M.S. On Trolley** Carrying the basket Komli climbs up to the river-bank towards Lalon. **The Camera tracks Lalon and brings him within the Frame.** **Komli**: There is something I want to discuss with you, Sain ... As she says this, Komli passes Lalon and starts moving ahead of him. **Komli**: Please come with me ... Komli starts walking. Lalon pursues her. **The Camera follows them.** After they have walked some distance. Komli speaks out while she is still moving— **Komli**: Tell me, Sain, can't I sing your songs? Lalon is taken by surprise with this strange question. He continues to walk without replying. **Komli**: Why don't you say something? **Lalon**: Your song makes a single flower bloom in four colours and raises a storm in a domain of emotions ... **Komli**: All these are merely your words of comfort to distract my mind, Sain.

CUT

SC No. SHOT DESCRIPTION & DIALOGUE

3 **M.C.S. On Trolley**

Komli puts down the basket from her head and advances towards Lalon.

Komli: Why didn't you initiate me as a disciple? … Why didn't you provide me with a companion for spiritual pursuit?

As she says this Komli's eyes fill with tears.

Lalon: How will I initiate you … You are the mother-figure of Shimultala … you are everybody's guardian …

Komli smiles briefly.

Komli: But my heart weeps, Sain … Who keeps note of that secret?

Lalon fondly places his hand on Komli's cheek.

Lalon: This touchiness does not become you, young Radhika … tomorrow it is you who will sing at the grand festival …

Komli: What shall I sing? Can I compose songs the way you do?

CUT

4 **M.L.S.**

Lalon starts singing –

Lalon (Song):

Blessed is he
Who has built a house, raising walls in emptiness …

CUT

'I search
myself ...
I search
human beings
And my
Guru Gosain
shows me
the way

SC No. SHOT DESCRIPTION & DIALOGUE

61 1 **Location: Hamlet at Shimultala**

Time : Morning

M.L.S. to M.S. On Crane

The Crane is at a height at the beginning of the Shot. While the music of the Prelude is in progress Shetal, Kalua and a few others enter on bamboo stilts and start dancing. **The Camera Crane is lowered.**

In the Foreground Komli is singing with a single-stringed lute raised above her head –

Komli (Song):

Blessed is he

who has built a house, raising walls in emptiness

Now everybody sings these two lines in chorus.

Chorus (Song):

Blessed is he

who has built a house raising walls in emptiness

CUT

KODAK

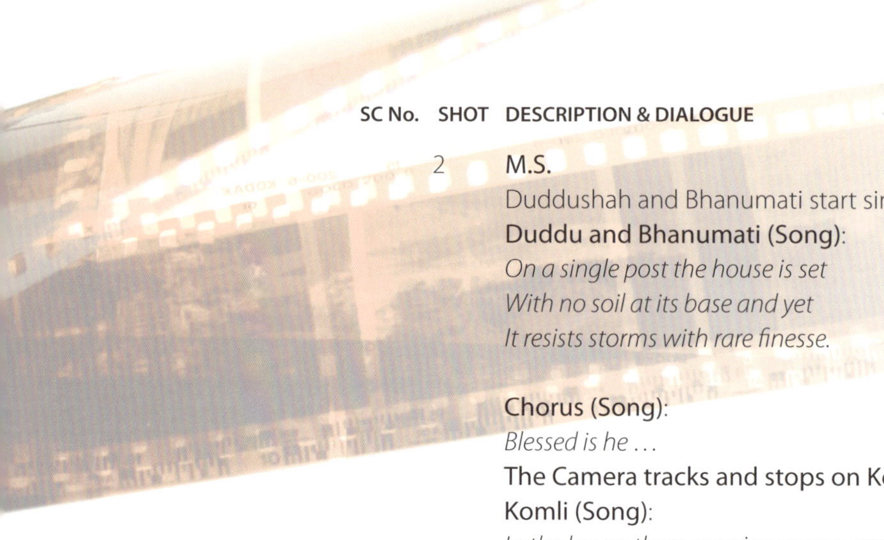

SC No. SHOT DESCRIPTION & DIALOGUE

2 M.S.

Duddushah and Bhanumati start singing.

Duddu and Bhanumati (Song):

On a single post the house is set
With no soil at its base and yet
It resists storms with rare finesse.

Chorus (Song):

Blessed is he . . .

The Camera tracks and stops on Komli and Bargakshepi.

Komli (Song):

In the house there are nine rooms spread in a cluster
And above them an attic finished in rough plaster

Bargakshepi (song):

There a mad fellow sits all alone with his Master.

CUT

3 M.S.

The men are dancing on bamboo stilts in the Background. Everyone is dancing and singing.

Chorus (Song):

Blessed is he . . .

Bargakshepi drags Mir Mosharraf and Harinath to the dancing platform.

CUT

4 **M.C.S. Low Angle Round Trolley**

Lalon (Song):
On top and bottom, side by side
There are nine and a half doors and still
Lalon says – I can go inside
Through any of them at will.
While singing Lalon walks out of the compound …

CUT

5 **L.S.**

All of them are dancing and advancing along the river-bank …
Chorus (Song):
Blessed is he …
The song comes to an end.

CUT

6 **M.S. Composite**

'Excellent! Well done!' cries are heard all around.
Mir Mosharraf, Ahmed Ali and Nitai Chandra Pal, who had come with Harinath are seen complimenting the performers.
Harinath: Fakir Sahib, let me introduce you to Nitai babu and Ahmed Ali. They have come from the estate of the zamindar of Atgharia to invite you there …

Lalon: Atgharia! The name sounds familiar. Isn't it somewhere in the Pabna area?

Nitai Chandra Pal: You are right. It is the Zamindary of Babu Sri Madhusudan Choudhury …

Lalon: I think I had gone there a long time back … with my Guru Siraj Sain …

CUT

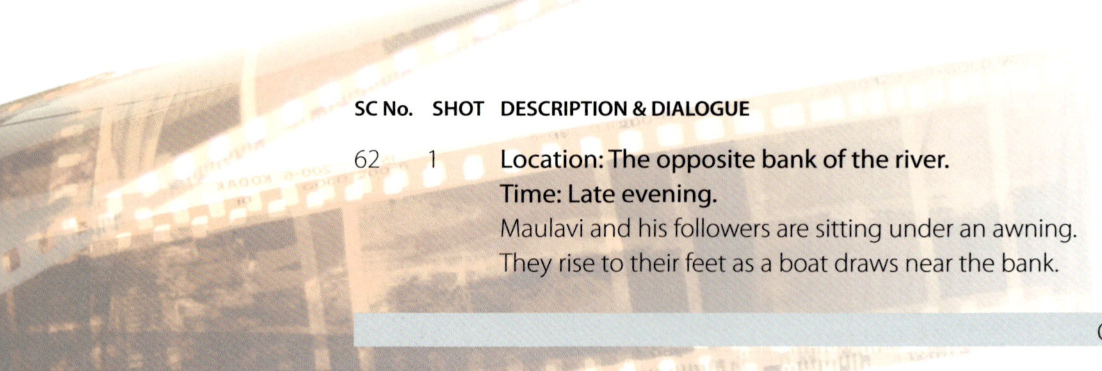

SC No.	SHOT	DESCRIPTION & DIALOGUE
62	1	**Location: The opposite bank of the river.** **Time: Late evening.** Maulavi and his followers are sitting under an awning. They rise to their feet as a boat draws near the bank.
		CUT
	2	**M.L.S. Long Focus lens** Kalua's small boat touches the bank. The boat is carrying Harinath, Mir Mosharraf and the Zamindar's representatives, Nitai Chandra Pal and Ahmed Ali. They alight from the boat. Maulavi had been waiting with some of his friends and followers. As soon as the boat reaches the bank they advance towards the boat quickly.
		CUT
	3	**M.S. Composite** As Kalua is tying the boat to a post, Maulavi says— **Maulavi**: We will go to the other bank … **Kalua**: Why, for what purpose? What business do you have there? **Maulavi**: That fellow—your Lalon Fakir … we want to have a debate with him. On hearing this last remark Harinath's group comes to a halt.

SC No. SHOT DESCRIPTION & DIALOGUE

Kalua: There won't be any debate today. We had songs and music all through the day at our hamlet. Fakir Sahib is exhausted ... You may call on us on some other day ...

One of the Maulavi's companions speaks out in a loud voice—

Companion: You people indulge in all sorts of forbidden activities in the name of holding your grand celebration!

Maulavi: All of you deserve to be condemned to hell!

Kalua: Have you come to threaten us, Maulavi Sahib?

Noting the rising excitement, Ahmed Ali draws near.

Ahmed Ali: I am Ahmed Ali ... an employee in the office of the Zamindar of Atgharia ...

Then pointing out at the gentleman standing next to him Ahmed Ali says –

Ahmed Ali: ... And this is Sri Nitai Chandra Pal, the Zamindar's Estate manager ...

The Maulavi's passion is deflated on hearing this. All of a sudden he turns very humble and makes his obeisance with utmost respect.

Nitai Chandra Pal: If you wish to have any debate or argument, come to Atgharia next Sunday. We have invited Lalon Fakir to hold a programme of songs,

Maulavi: Yes, sir.

The Maulavi starts walking away with his men.

CUT

SC No.	SHOT	DESCRIPTION & DIALOGUE
	4	**M.C.S. Composite** Harinath and Mir Mosharraf advance towards the pathway above the river-bank. **Harinath**: What did you make of all this, Mir bhaiya? The situation seems to be getting somewhat complicated … **Mir Mosharraf**: Nothing serious … it is the same old story– religious arguments with occasional disputes and conflict …
		CUT
	5	**M.S. Composite On Trolley** Maulavi, visibly angry, is going back with his men. Harinath, Mir Mosharraf and a little behind them— Ahmed Ali and Nitai Chandra Pal are seen in the Background. **Maulavi**: Come, let us all go to Atgharia. Go and inform Shastri Moshai. We must strip these shameless imposters stark naked in front of the entire gathering of villagers …
		CUT

SC No.	SHOT	DESCRIPTION & DIALOGUE
63	1	**Location: A stage set up for the programme on the bank of a large tank in Atgharia.** **Time: Morning** **M.C.S On Trolley** **The Camera is tracking.** Various musical instruments, one-stringed and two-stringed lutes, tabours etcetera are being tuned. Lalon, Duddu, Bholai, Kalua, Maniruddin, Komli, Bargakshepi and Bhanumati are on the stage.

CUT

2 **M.S. On Trolley**

Ahmed Ali and Harinath are advancing towards a group of people in the Foreground. A crowded gathering of villagers is seen in the Background.

More people are arriving to attend the programme.

Shastri Moshai and other Brahmins are sitting on one side.

Maulavi and his followers are sitting on the opposite side.

Ahmed Ali approaches them and says —

Ahmed Ali: You may finish your debate and argument session before the Zamindar babu arrives here. Lalon Sain is agreeable to this suggestion …

Both parties consent to this.

Now Harinath turns towards the audience and says—

Harinath: Dear brothers, mothers and sisters—we have arranged to hold a debate before the commencement of songs and music. Shastri Moshai is here and so is Maulavi Sahib … they wish to hold a debate with Lalon Fakir. Let us listen to them …

CUT

3 **M.L.S.**

Ahmed Ali is standing in the Foreground. The spectators are seen in the Background. Separate seating arrangements have been allotted for men and women. A curtain has been hung between the two areas. There is a rising murmur among the spectators.

Spectators: Let the singing be held first …
A second group of spectators says –
Second group: Songs first, debate later …
Harinath looks discomfited in the Foreground.

CUT

4 **M.S.**
Raising his hand holding a single-stringed lute, Lalon gestures to the spectators to stay calm.
Voices are raised from Off Frame.
Spectators: Let us have a song, Sainji …
Lalon starts singing a song in light humour –
Lalon (Song):
Unknowingly I tasted a wild arum and now
I must get some tamarind right away somehow …
The laughter of the audience is heard …

CUT

5 **M.S.Composite**

Lalon is in the Foreground. The spectators are in front.

Lalon (song):

Arum has a terrible itch, as everyone knows,
But this I had sadly failed to diagnose.
Now I am driven mad by its burning trek,
My throat's itching without a moment's break.

CUT

6 **M.S.**

The spectators burst out in loud laughter.

One spectator: Let's hear one more, Sainji ...

CUT

7 **Lalon**: Yes, there will be songs, many songs ... that is why we have all come here ...

But two distinguished scholars, *Shastri Moshai and *Maulavi Sahib are here to hold a debate with an utterly ignorant man like me ...

* Shastri Moshai : A title given to a scholar versed in Hindu scriptures

* Maulavi Sahib: Islamic scholar or teacher

SC No. SHOT DESCRIPTION & DIALOGUE

Do accept my humble obeisance Shastri Moshai … I salute you, Maulavi Sahib … please start …

CUT

8 **M.S. Low Angle**

Shastri Moshai looks this way and that and then rises to his feet.

Shastri Moshai: You call yourself an ascetic. And yet your songs carry stinging insinuations about our ancient myths; you cry fie upon our caste-system which has been prevailing for centuries … you refute the rulings handed down by *Manu* … Is this devotion or sacrilege? Answer me …

CUT

9 **M.S.**

Lalon answers in a calm voice –

Lalon: Who says that I am an ascetic? I am a most ordinary man … I search myself … I search human beings … and my Guru Gosain shows me the way. Who am I to speak of myths and scriptures? Those words were spoken by Gour Nitai! Gourchand came to Nadia and composed new laws in which myths and scriptures were excluded. He saw no difference in caste, creed or religion … he believed solely in the rites of pure adoration … and it is only his words which I recount to others …

Finishing his speech, Lalon folds his hands on his forehead.

CUT

10 **M.S.**

Shastri Moshai is taken aback by Lalon's remarks.

Then he raises his voice and says—

Shastri Moshai: Is that a proper reply to my question?

Then he again looks this way and that before saying—

Shastri Moshai: What do you think, Maulavi Sahib?

SC No. SHOT DESCRIPTION & DIALOGUE

Maulavi almost jumps up to his feet—

Maulavi: In the name of celebrating a grand festival all you people do is dance and sing! You also smoke opium and *_bhang_—all these are absolutey forbidden activities . . .

CUT

11 **M.S. to M.C.S. On Trolley**

Lalon: If our songs are unwarranted, why then did the Maulavi Sahibs listen with overwhelming interest to the *ghazal*s and *masnabir*s sung at religious gatherings by ardent devotees like Maulana Rumi Hafez, Moinuddin Chisti and Zamir? Is it blasphemy only when sung in Bengali?

The Camera tracks to reach Close to Lalon.

CUT

12 **M.S.**

Maulavi and Shastri Moshai are standing. Maulavi is almost deflated, but he regains his self-confidence and says in a forceful tone—

Maulavi: He is insulting the Muslims, he is an infidel . . . he does not go by the *Shariah . . .

A murmur is heard in the audience.

CUT

13 **M.C.S.**

Lalon again speaks in a calm voice—

Lalon: Listen, Maulavi sahib, you are an educated man . . . tell me, is it possible to skip the vowels and learn the consonants? Similarly, it is not possible to form any religious concept without learning the rituals. Rituals and concept are like milk and butter. Remove the butter and what is left is . . . whey! This is known to everyone . . .

CUT

* Bhang: Preparation from the extract of leaves and flowers of the cannabis plant, smoked or consumed as a drink in the Indian sub-continent

* Shariah: Islamic laws

SC No.	SHOT	DESCRIPTION & DIALOGUE

14 **M.L.S.**

A suppressed murmur is again heard in the audience from Lalon's P.O.V. Maulavi raises his voice and says—

Maulavi: He is trying to evade the topic of the debate. There is only one query that I wish to raise before this august gathering—is he a Hundu or a Muslim?

CUT

15 Ahmed Ali and Harinath look disturbed as they hastily rise to their feet.

CUT

16 **M.S. to M.C.S. On Trolley Crane**

Lalon replies to the Maulavi's query in a calm and composed manner. **From Low Angle the Camera rises to Lalon's M.C.S.**

Lalon (Song):

Everyone asks what is Lalon's religion
As he walks barefoot on earth
Lalon says – what does religion look like –
I haven't seen it since my birth …

CUT

17 **M.S.**

Ahmed Ali enters the Frame and advances towards Shastri Moshai and Maulavi.

Ahmed Ali: Please stop this. We have had enough of this debate. Now let us have some songs. The Master is due to arrive soon.

Shastri Moshai is furious and he now tries to excite the crowd as he says—

Shastri Moshai: Are you aware that this man grabs chaste women from the cemetery and keeps them in his hamlet? And what is more—he gets Brahmin widows married to Muslim men … men and women co-habit in his hamlet like animals. Each of those females that you see is a harlot. All these are highly immoral practices!

SC No.	SHOT	DESCRIPTION & DIALOGUE
		Maulavi: Yes, this self-styled fakir has got hold of all those women of loose morals and opened a den of hell …
		CUT
	18	**M.S. (Toppish)** In a section of the audience a few robust youths are seen taking out their hidden sticks, choppers etcetera.
		CUT
	19	**C.S.** Now Bhanumati, Komli and Bargakshepi rise to their feet one by one. Bargakshepi addresses Bhanumati—
		CUT
	20	**M.S. Composite** Bargakshepi, Komli and Bhanumati. Bargakshepi tells Bhanumati— **Bargakshepi**: You can start, Bhanti …

SC No. SHOT DESCRIPTION & DIALOGUE

Bhanumati: These people had planned to burn me alive. Sainji rescued me. He is our God. Our village is like a heaven to us. We are living there like proper human beings.

Komli: They said that we are fallen women—immoral characters. But who has made us fall? High-born Brahmins like you. I was a Brahmin widow. My husband had ten other wives. If a high-born Brahmin can live with ten wives, why can't I co-habit with more than one man? How many husbands did Draupadi have in the *Mahabharata*? Tell me …

CUT

21 **M.C.S.**

Shastri Moshai turns around and addresses the spectators in an attempt to provoke them –

Shastri Moshai: All of you just heard what this wretched woman said. She admitted on her own that she is a depraved character, she co-habits with several men …

CUT

22 **M.C.S. on Trolley**

Bargakshepi: Here, you lewd Brahmin! Whom are you calling depraved? Do you recognise me? Listen, all of you—I was born in a Muslim family. When my husband died this lewd fellow had taken advantage of me and raped me … But you didn't make any religious distinction at that time! Why? Did you lose your sense of judgement altogether in the heat of your excitement?

CUT

23 **M.S.**

Shastri Moshai's face, turned pale, is seen in the Foreground. The spectators are seen and it is noticed that they have grown a little restless. Abruptly bricks and brickbats start getting hurled in the direction of the stage from a particular corner.

CUT

24 **M.S.**

The stage is being struck by bricks. While Lalon is shielding the women and taking them away he is hit by a stone on his forehead. Blood starts pouring from his forehead.

CUT

25 **M.S. to M. L.S.**

Kalua jumps down from the stage. Pushing away the spectators he runs in the direction from where the bricks are being hurled.

CUT

26 **M.S. On Crane**

Kalua arrives in the midst of the hooligans.

Kalua: Where is the bastard who is hurling stones?

As he says this Kalua grabs one of the men by his throat.

Now getting Kalua all alone among them the hooligans start beating him up mercilessly. Komli is seen to come running in that direction. One of the hooligans raises his chopper threateningly. The villagers start running away.

CUT

27 **M.S. to M.C.S. On Trolley**
Harinath and Nitai babu start running in the direction of the Zamindar's mansion.

CUT

28 Shielding Lalon, who is bleeding profusely, Ahmed Ali takes him away from the stage.
Bhanumati and Duddu follow them.

CUT

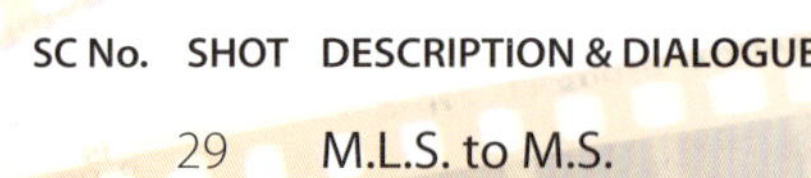

SC No.	SHOT	DESCRIPTION & DIALOGUE

29 **M.L.S. to M.S.**

Harinath is standing near a staircase inside the Zamindar's mansion. Nitai babu is seen coming down a private staircase. Zamindar Madhusudan Choudhury comes down the same staircase. He looks very angry.

Zamindar: Beat up those rowdy hooligans and crack their heads …

The Zamindar's footmen and guards, armed with spears, battle-axes and sticks are seen in the Foreground.

Zamindar: How dare they resort to all this hooliganism within my land! Break their arms and legs and lock them up … Go …

CUT

30 **M.S. to M.C.S.**

The hooligans start having fun with Komli and Bargakshepi. They tug at their hair, try to pull off their clothes and violate their modesty. Bargakshepi starts slapping the rogues and pinching them.

CUT

SC No.	SHOT	DESCRIPTION & DIALOGUE

31 **M.L.S. (Toppish) On Crane**

The Zamindar's footmen and guards attack the hooligans. The bewildered spectators start running helter skelter.

The hooligans who had come from outside are now scared and they try to make their escape.

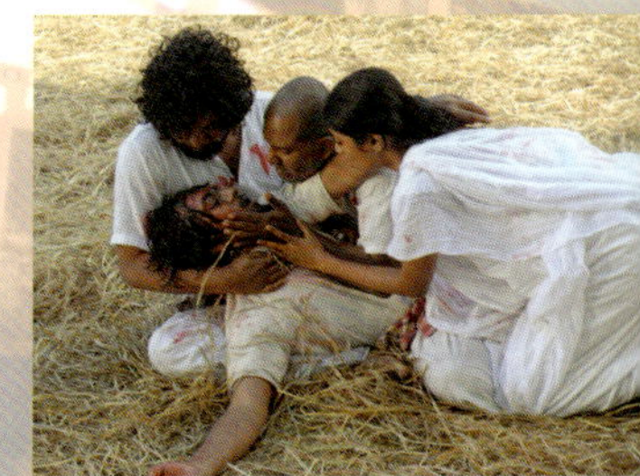

CUT

32 **M.C.S. Composite On Trolley**

By the side of a pond Bhanumati is pressing the edge of her sari to Lalon's forehead for stopping the flow of blood. Her white sari is soaked in blood. The noise of the disturbance is heard from a distance.

CUT

33 **M.L.S. (Toppish) 120° On Crane**

Maulavi and Shastri Moshai are trying to find a place near the pond where they can hide.

CUT

34 **The Camera Crane is lowered to reach 90° toppish position.**

Kalua is lying on the ground. Komli and Bargakshepi try to lift him up. Their white saris are soaked in blood. Lalon enters the Frame. Lalon lifts up Kalua in his arms.

CUT

35 **M.S. to M.C.S.**

Lalon is carrying Kalua, who is bleeding profusely. Kalua has been dealt a sharp blow with a chopper on his throat, which has rendered him speechless.

An inarticulate sound escapes his lips—

Kalua: Friend …

CUT

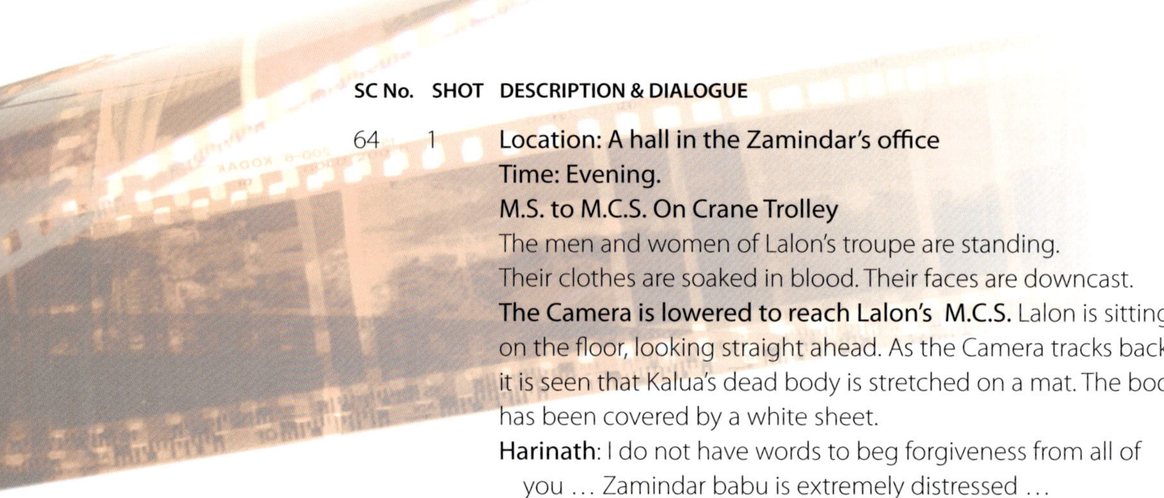

SC No.	SHOT	DESCRIPTION & DIALOGUE
64	1	**Location: A hall in the Zamindar's office** **Time: Evening.** **M.S. to M.C.S. On Crane Trolley** The men and women of Lalon's troupe are standing. Their clothes are soaked in blood. Their faces are downcast. **The Camera is lowered to reach Lalon's M.C.S.** Lalon is sitting on the floor, looking straight ahead. As the Camera tracks back it is seen that Kalua's dead body is stretched on a mat. The body has been covered by a white sheet. **Harinath**: I do not have words to beg forgiveness from all of you … Zamindar babu is extremely distressed …
		CUT
	2	**M.S. Composite** Zamindar babu is seated on a chair. Nitai babu and Harinath are standing next to him. Ahmed Ali stands a little away from them. Footmen and guards carrying arms are standing behind the group. **Zamindar**: But you people can rest assured that we are holding the miscreants in our custody. They will be caned in public and then handed over to the police. Death penalty is what they deserve.
		CUT

SC No.	SHOT	DESCRIPTION & DIALOGUE
	3	**M.S. Composite** **Lalon in Foreground. The members of his troupe are Out of Focus behind him.** **Lalon**: Please forgive them, Babu Moshai. They have been denied the advantage of good company, they have no Guru to guide them … they are a confused lot. Without a guide how can they make out the seven levers?

CUT

SC No.	SHOT	DESCRIPTION & DIALOGUE
65	1	**Location: A river in a dream** **Time: A misty morning** **M.L.S.** With the commencement of music a boat is seen to advance, piercing the mist. A song is sung in the Background. **Song**: *Heigh ho! Heigh ho! Heigh ho!* *Only when you pierce the seven levers, my friend* *You can pierce the chamber of the wind in the end.* *Once in the wind-chamber you can* *Easily get hold of the elusive man.* *Then, matching the wind with the wind, oh mind,* *As you float along with the tide you will find* *The water shall freely let you through* *So long as the Guru's blessings are with you.* Men and women are seen rowing the boat in unison.
		MIX
	2	**M.L.S. (Toppish)** The boat enters the Frame. Kalua's body has been laid down in the middle of the boat. Lalon is at the helm. The others are rowing.
		MIX
	3	**M.S. Low Angle** **The Camera is at water-level.** Lalon is steering the helm.
		MIX
	4	**M.S. (Same as Sh-3)** Now Siraj Sain is seen steering the helm.
		MIX

SC No.	SHOT	DESCRIPTION & DIALOGUE
	5	**M.L.S.** A large flock of countless migratory birds fly by.
		MIX
	6	**M.L.S. (Tracking from the boat)** The dream boat is moving on.
		MIX
	7	**Shot 6 M.L.S. (Tracking from the boat)** The dream boat moves away through a creek.
		CUT

The Director steers: All set for shooting the dream boat sequence

66 1 **Location: Bungalow at Silaidaha**
Time: Night
C.S.
Lalon: This is how the boat symbolising our life continues to float in joy and sorrow – my Guru is my steersman, he whispers in my ears all the time – 'speak the truth and follow the path of virtue; if you cannot recognise truth and virtue; you will never be able to discover the true identity of human beings'. And so, you can see—how I have had the good fortune of meeting a person like you.

CUT

2 **Jyotirindranath**: You have opened up my eyes. I had no idea that such treasure troves existed within our estate …
Then Jyotirindranath speaks to Lalon in a courteous voice—
Jyotirindranath: Please tell me—what can I do for you people?

CUT

3 Jyotirindranath and Lalon.
Lalon: We are a small group of people, miserably poor and thrown out by society … We did not know that the hamlet that we have built in the forest falls within the purview of your estate. We had thought that forests, woods, rivers, canals and marshes – all these were the property of the Creator …

The Zamindar's steward is seen walking down the veranda.

Jyotirindranath: What you thought was natural.

We, zamindars have used our force to split up all that property among ourselves. Perhaps not even the tiniest bit of land is left under the Creator's custody anywhere on the face of this earth today.

CUT

SC No.	SHOT	DESCRIPTION & DIALOGUE

4 Then Jyotirindranath addresses his steward and says –

Jyotirindranath: Sachin babu, draw up a deed assigning this Fakir sahib's village as tax-free land … and please make sure that the signing of the document and other formalities are completed while I am here …

CUT

5 **M.S.**

Sachin babu: Sir, I am making all necessary arrangements … please do not worry.

Then Sachin babu addresses Lalon and says –

Sachin babu: Fakir sahib, a young man and his wife have been waiting for a long time to see you … he says his name is Gagan … I did not wish to disturb you in the midst of your discussions.

CUT

6 **M.S. COMPOSITE On Trolley**

Lalon speaks out anxiously –

Lalon: Gagan is here! Permit me to take leave of you, Babu Moshai … I had given him my word … Gagan Harkara … he delivers mail and composes songs as well … I have a mind to spend the rest of the night at his hut.

While talking Lalon stretches his hands towards his bag and his lute.

Sachin babu goes out and waits in the veranda.

CUT

7 **M.S.**

Lalon: I do not have words to thank you …

Jyotirindranath rises to his feet. **The Camera tracks to Compose Jyotirindranath and Lalon.**

Jyotirindranath: Do keep a little space for me in your village in the forest … Maybe, one day I will build a small hut and start living there.

SC No.	SHOT	DESCRIPTION & DIALOGUE
		For all these days I was unaware that we had a neighbour like you … this was our great misfortune!
		CUT
	8	Lalon breaks into a song— **Lalon (Song):** *I haven't seen him a single day.* *In a town of mirrors close to where I stay* *He is among the many neighbours who dwell* *Under a single roof and are yet faring well …* *I haven't seen him a single day …*
		CUT
	9	Lalon smiles briefly and then putting the lute back in his bag he starts walking. Jyotirindranath remains standing at the same spot. Sachin babu and Lalon are out of the Frame. Jyotirindranath approaches the piano, sits down and picks up a chord.
		CUT

67 1 **Location: Gagan's dilapidated hut.**

Time: Night

M.S. to C.S. On Trolley

Moving above Gagan's wife the Camera tracks to reach Gagan. In the dim light they are seen sitting together in the hut and singing. Gagan is singing without the accompaniment of any music—

Gagan (Song):

Where will I find the one
whom my heart craves in bitter pain . . .
Having lost him, here and there I run
searching everywhere, but all in vain . . .

The Camera tracks to come close to Lalon.

Gagan: Forgive me, if I am mistaken, Sainji, but it was you who had told me once that Gagan searches for the one whom his heart craves for.

Lalon: The one whom the heart craves for! But I haven't found him yet … Would I at all be able to find him in this life?

Lalon's eyes start glistening with tears.

DISSOLVE

68 1 **Location: Gagan's hut**

Time: Dawn

M.L.S. (Toppish)

It is dawn. Old Lalon comes out very slowly from Gagan's thatched hut and stands in the courtyard.

A Muezzin's call to attend early morning prayers comes floating from a distance.

MIX

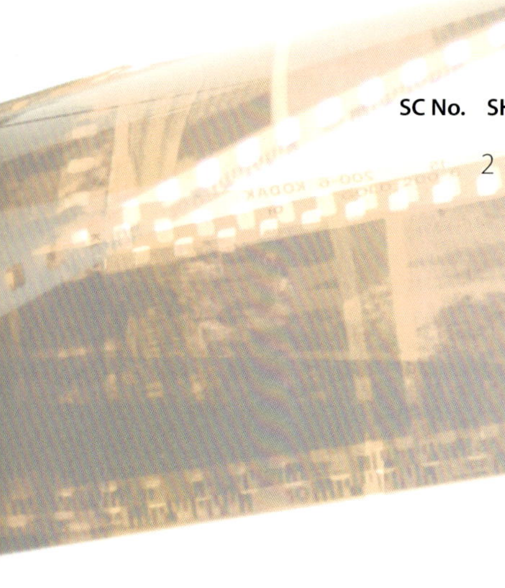

SC No.	SHOT	DESCRIPTION & DIALOGUE

2 **M.L.S. to M.S. On Trolley**

Standing in the pleasant glow of dawn Lalon is looking at the horizon. His eyes seem to be searching for some one. In a slightly slow motion Gagan's wife enters the Frame with a single-stringed lute in her hand.

Lalon seems to be engrossed in a dream. Unconsciously Lalon takes the lute from Gagan's wife. **The Camera Tracks back a little**. A song emerges from Lalon's lips –

Lalon (Song):

When shall I be united with the single entity
For whom my heart pines with such intensity

With the lute in upraised hands Lalon goes on singing and tapping his foot in time with the song.

CUT

3 **M.S.**

Lalon, Gagan and his wife. Now the singing commences in rhythm.

Song:

When shall I be united with the single entity
For whom my heart pines with such intensity.
Like a thirsty cuckoo I fix my sight
On the dark moon as I pine all night
To serve at the feet of the one I adore–
Alas, my fate denies me, as I was denied before ...

CUT

4 **M.S. to L.S. On long Crane**

Toppish Shot shows that in a little Slow motion all three are dancing in a frenzied manner. **The Camera Crane is lifted.** The sun is rising in the horizon, its reflected image on the river water. All three of them have become engrossed in a frenzy of emotional turmoil as they dance with uplifted arms.

The next lines of the song are heard in chorus.

The Camera goes on rising. End Title Role is raised.

SC No. SHOT DESCRIPTION & DIALOGUE

Song:

Just as a lightning streak
covered by cloud is seen no more
So, having lost the one I seek
on this mirror I see the image I adore.
When shall I be united with the single entity
for whom my heart pines with such intensity.

ROLL UP TITLE CARDS

FADE OUT

Characters Unmasked

Jyotirindranath Tagore (Priyanshu Chatterjee)

Old Lalon (Prosenjit Chattopadhyay)

Young Lalon (Naufel Jishan)

Lalon's wife Golapi (Tathoi)

Lalon's mother Padmabati (Gulshan Ara Champa)

Kabiraj (Hasan Imam)

Bina (Deepa Poddar)

Siraj Sai (Raisul Islam Asad)

Kabiraj's wife (Layla Hasan)

Rabeya (Rokeya Prachee)

Kalimuddin (Asanul Haque Minu)

Kalua (Chanchal Chowdhury)

Komli (Paoli Dam)

Hindu priest (Shanu Banerjee)

Moulavi (Amir Shirazi)

Harinath Mazumdar (Shantilal Mukherjee)

Mir Mosharraf Hussain (Anirban Guha)

Duddu Shah (Shahed Ali)

Bargakshepi (Bibi Russell)

Bhanumati (Shuvra Kundu)

Behind the Screen

Story: Sunil Gangopadhyay

Script/Direction/Cinematography/Music/Choreography: Goutam Ghose

Production: An Indo-Bangladesh co-production
Goutam Kundu (Rosevalley Films Pvt. Ltd.), Habibur Rahman Khan (Ashirbad Cholochhitra), Faridpur Reza Sagar (Impress Telefilm Ltd.)

Editing: Moloy Banerjee

Production Designer: Samir Chanda

Art Direction: Mohinuddin Faruque & Somnath Pakre

Sound Designer: Anup Mukhopadhyay, Anirban Sengupta and Dipankar Chaku.

Make up: Vikram Gaikwad

Costume Designer: Neelanjana Ghose & Bibi Russell

Songs written by: Lalon Fakir, Shahjad Firdaus, Shah Alam

Line Production: Shah Alam Kiran & Kalyan Dasgupta

Executive Producers: Goutam Sarkar & Shihab Ahmad Shiraji

Production Controller: Shanu Banerjee

Stills: Abhijit Kundu & Rafiqul Islam Rustam

Songs rendered by: Farida Parveen, Abdul Latif Shah, Surajit Burman, Golam Faqir, Sourabh Mondal, Antara Chowdhury, Chandana Majumdar, Kalikaprasad, Rajib Das, Upali Chattopadhyay, Enakshi Bhattacharya, Pallab Ghosh.

Cast: Prosenjit Chattopadhyay, Raisul Islam Asad, Paoli Dam, Shubhra Kundu, Chanchal Chowdhury, Hasan Imam, Priyanshu Chatterjee, Jishan, Gulshan Ara Champa, Tathoi, Layla Hasan, Deepa Poddar, Shormi, Shantilal Mukherjee, Anirban Guha, Sourabh Mondal, Shanu Banerjee, Rokeya Prachee, Shankar Debnath, Tamal Mukherjee, Goutam Mukherjee, Bhaskar Bandopadhyay, and others.

Distribution: Rosevalley Films (India) in association with Venkatesh Films, Ashirbad Cholochhitra (Bangladesh)

Technical Details: 35 mm, Fujicolor, Dolby Digital, 150 minutes

Release: 3rd December, 2010 (in India and Bangladesh)

Reviews

A movie invariably lays claim to contemporaneousness, even if it is based on a thousand-year old anecdote. It is amazing how Goutam Ghose has created a unique character out of Sunil Gangopadhyay's novel *Moner Manush* at a time when the subcontinent is reeling under terrorism and diverse political forces are bent on destroying the communal harmony between Hindus and Muslims. There is a lot that can be written about this movie. From beginning to end it provides an experience of viewing a film of international standard. And like Lalon, Goutam Ghose too must have had to search long and hard for finding Chheunrhia, set in the midst of marshes and rivers and those rare men who had devoted their lives in quest of the one and only entity their heart craved for.

Moner Manush will serve as a gospel to those who worship the religion of humanity.

Mamunur Rashid
(Renowned playwright)
Pratham Alo (Daily newspaper), Dhaka
9th December, 2010

My expectation that Goutam Ghose's film on Sunil Gangopadhyay's historical novel, *Moner Manush* would be a unique work of art was fulfilled while I saw the film. When the movie came to an end, it seemed as if I had been rudely woken up from a wonderful dream. Defying all logic my conscious spirit \was seized by a strong urge to return to that dream. For two and a half hours I had remained immersed in transcendental pleasure amidst stretching forests and flowing rivers, brilliantly captured by the camera and among simple men and women living under the open sky, their lives dedicated to their love for God and their fondness for each other, singing,

dancing and rejoicing in divine glory with an unfathomable intensity. It was a truly wonderful experience.

Non-believers among us tend to ignore the eternal truth and think that the Almighty and ever-merciful God is an imaginary entity, born from our extreme fear of death. But in *Moner Manush* even that imaginary image is lit up by a melody of songs through the calm and compassionate expression in Lalon Fakir's eyes, which brings forth promises of everlasting joy in another world beyond this life. The movie, judged from its true significance then assumes the status of a religious gospel, earning its right to be placed alongside the works of Nanak, Kabir and other saints of the past.

Tapan Roychoudhury
(Eminent historian, Professor Emeritus,
Oxford University)
Desh (Fortnightly journal)
Kolkata, 17th December, 2010